"WORKS TO SUGGEST THAT THE ACT FINALLY DISTILLS INTO SOMETHING DENSE AND UNKNOWABLE"
Illegal Alien's
Guide to Critical Theory

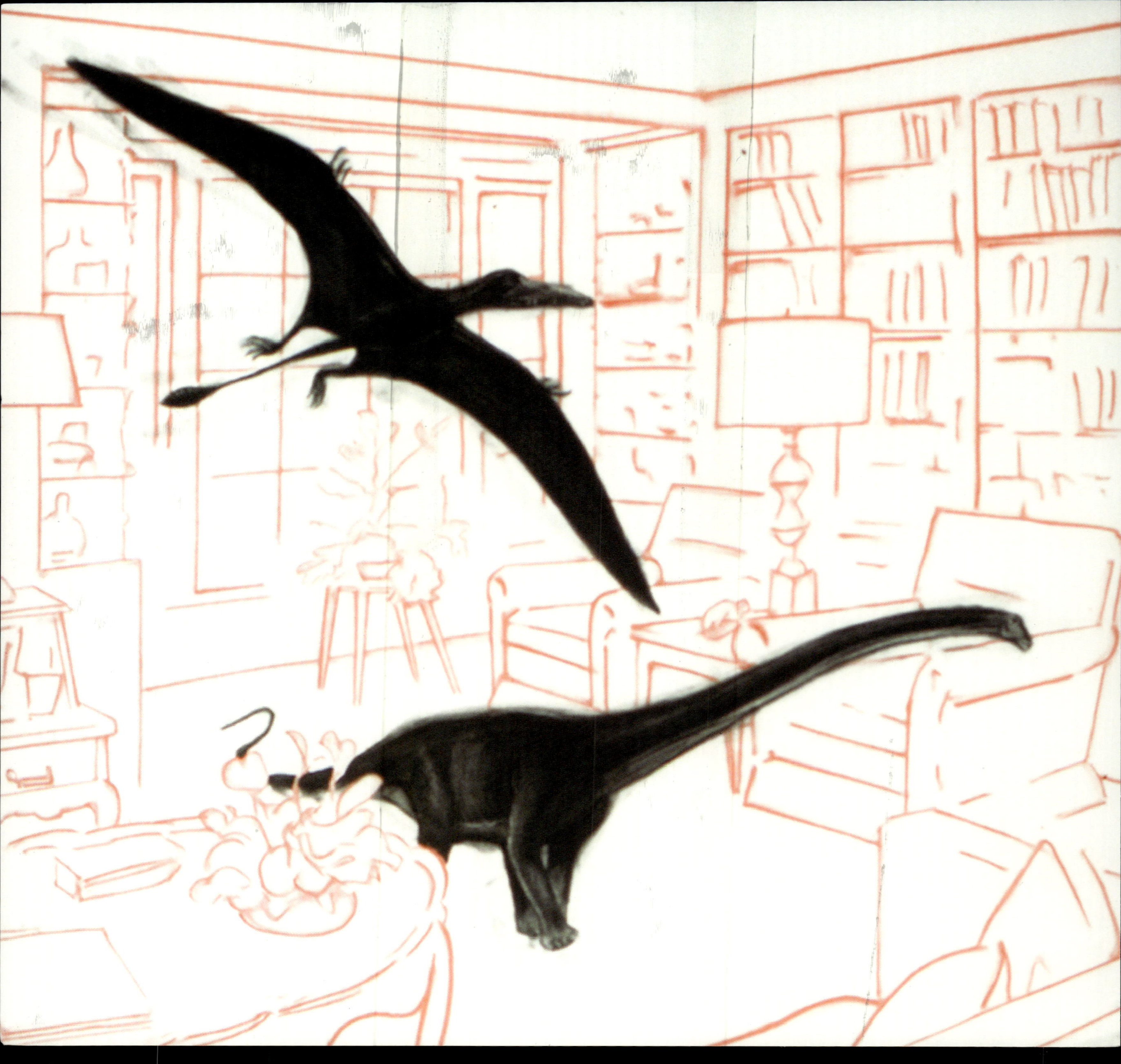

ALIeNS

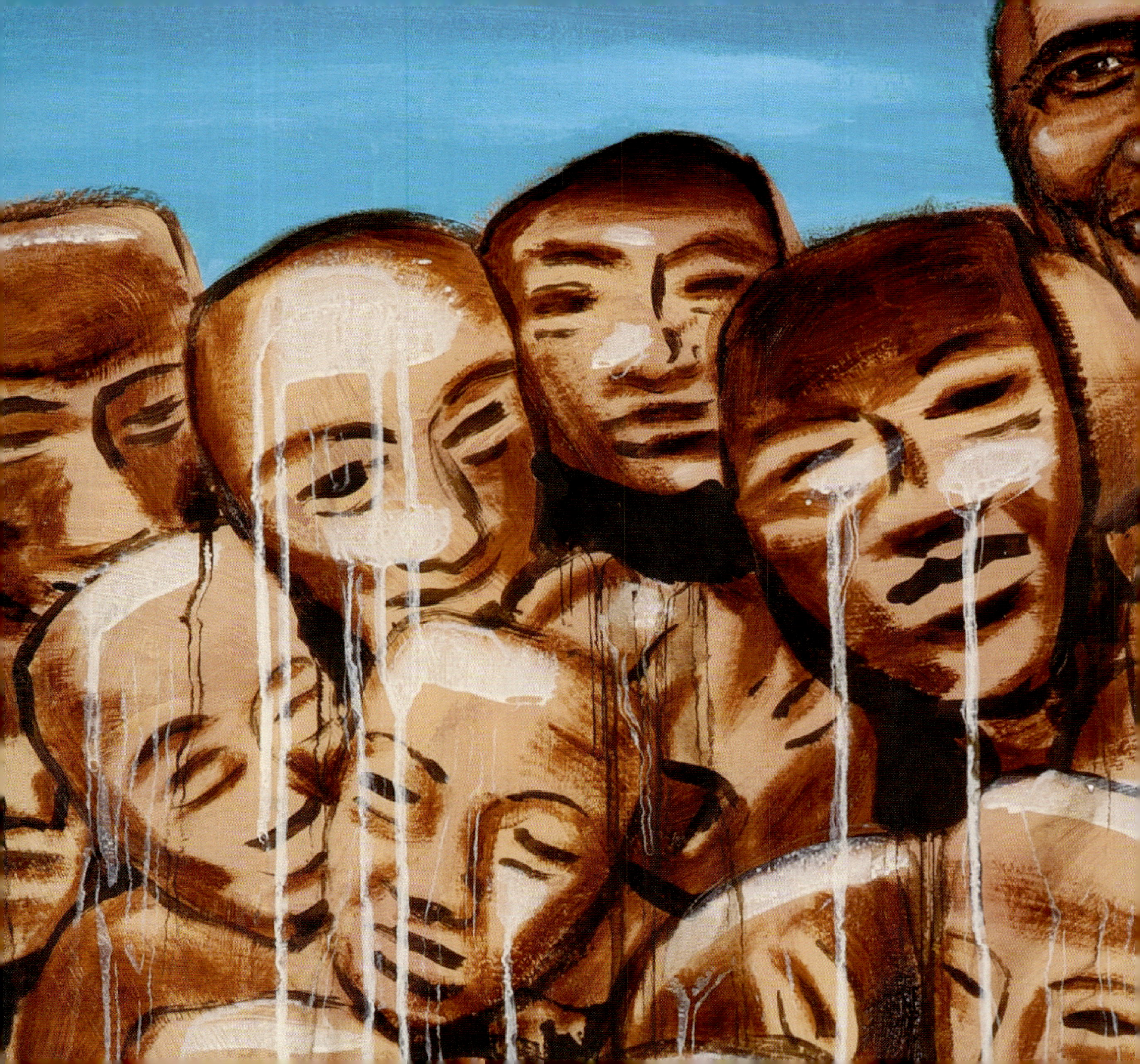

ALIeNS

Art and Text by Enrique Chagoya

Edited by Bart Schneider

Kelly's Cove Press

Published by Kelly's Cove Press
Berkeley, California

www.kellyscovepress.com

Published in the United States of America

ISBN 978-0-9891664-9-2

Library of Congress Control Number: 2018963687

FIRST EDITION

Cover and interior design by Lynn Phelps

Cover: *The Day After* (Detail), 2018, acrylic and water based oil on canvas. 16 x 20 in.

Back cover: *Illegal Alien's School of Art and Architecture* (Detail), 2006, acrylic, water based oil, solvent transfers and wood. 11 ½ x 108 ½ in.

Front endpaper: *Illegal Alien's Guide to Critical Theory* (Detail), 2007, color lithograph. 24 x 40 in.

Painting adjacent to the half-title page: *Liberty* (Detail), 2006, charcoal and pastel on paper mounted on canvas. 48 x 48 in.

Painting adjacent to title page: *Dreamers* (Detail), 2013, acrylic and water based oil on Amate paper mounted on canvas. 48 x 48 in.

Painting adjacent to back half-title page: *Illegal Alien's Guide to the Surplus of Nothingness* (Detail), 2009, acrylic, water based oil and decals. 12 x 82 in.

Back endpaper: *Then and Now: Aliens Sans Frontières* (Detail), 2018, acrylic, water based oil, solvent transfers, typeset in Farsi, decals, collaged glass eyes and wood. 11 1/2 x 108 1/2 in.

All text by Enrique Chagoya, from a conversation with Bart Schneider, August, 2018.

This book was published with financial support from the School of Humanities and Sciences Dean's Office at Stanford University.

10 9 8 7 6 5 4 3 2 1

A good citizen is somebody who respects people for their differences. Personally, I feel that I am a citizen of a borderless country and I know people who are also from that country. These are people who generally have experience moving from one place to another. My experiences have made me realize that I am from everywhere and from nowhere.

ALIENS

I believe that everybody is an alien. I think that we all come from somewhere else. Nobody is pure ethnically. Those times are gone. Maybe there was never any purity in human history in terms of ethnicity because we are all part of the same genome. Recently I searched for my own DNA history through one of the services. I'm 38% Native American from Central Mexico, 28% Iberian or Southern European, probably from Spain, and the remaining 44% includes forebearers who were Ashkenazi Jews, Middle Eastern Arabs, as well as others from North Africa and Asia. My ancestors were promiscuous. They traveled and mixed with other ethnic groups.

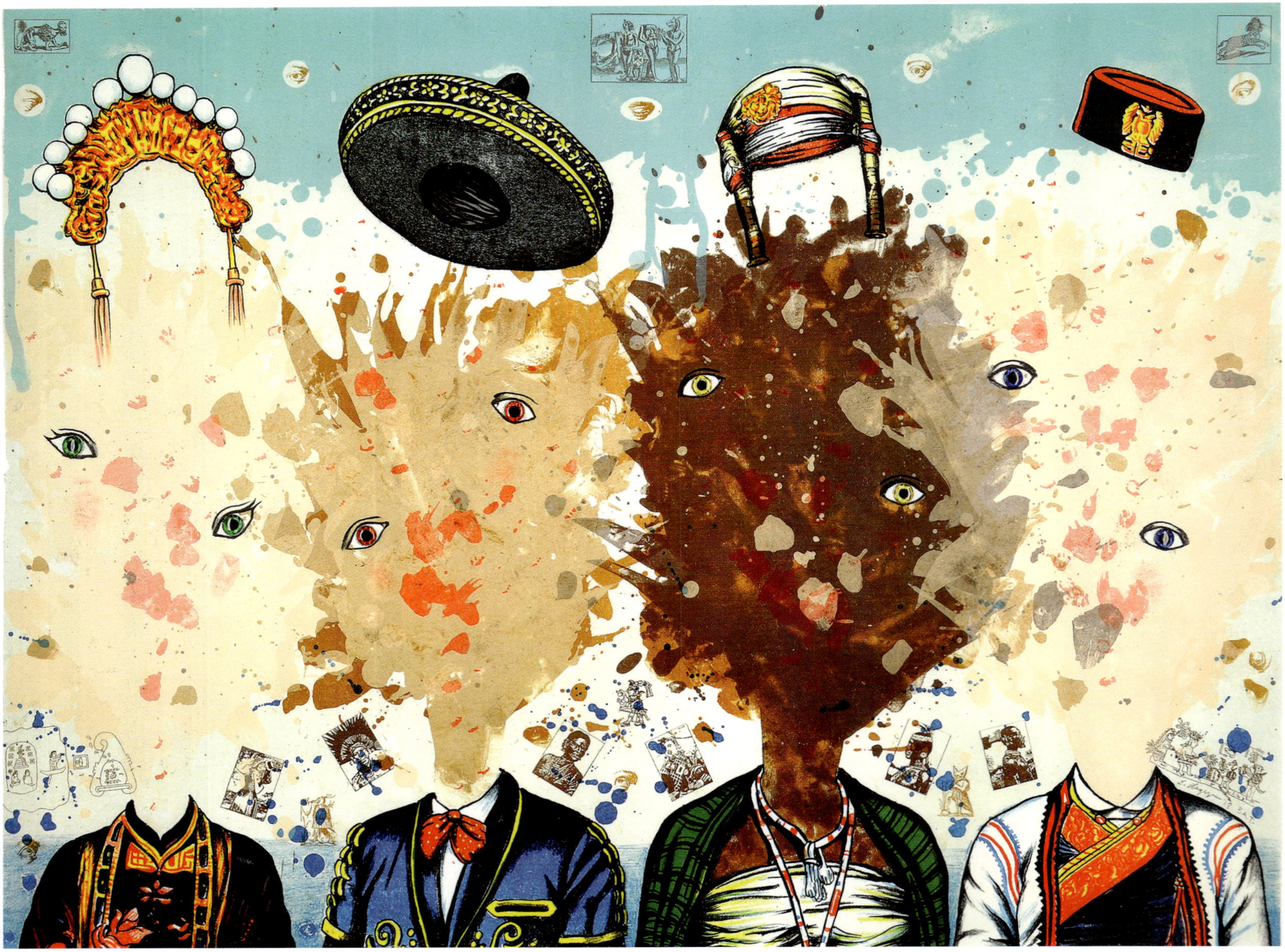

Everyone is an Alienígeno, 2018
20-color lithograph and plastic eye stickers on handmade Amate paper. 22 x 30 in.

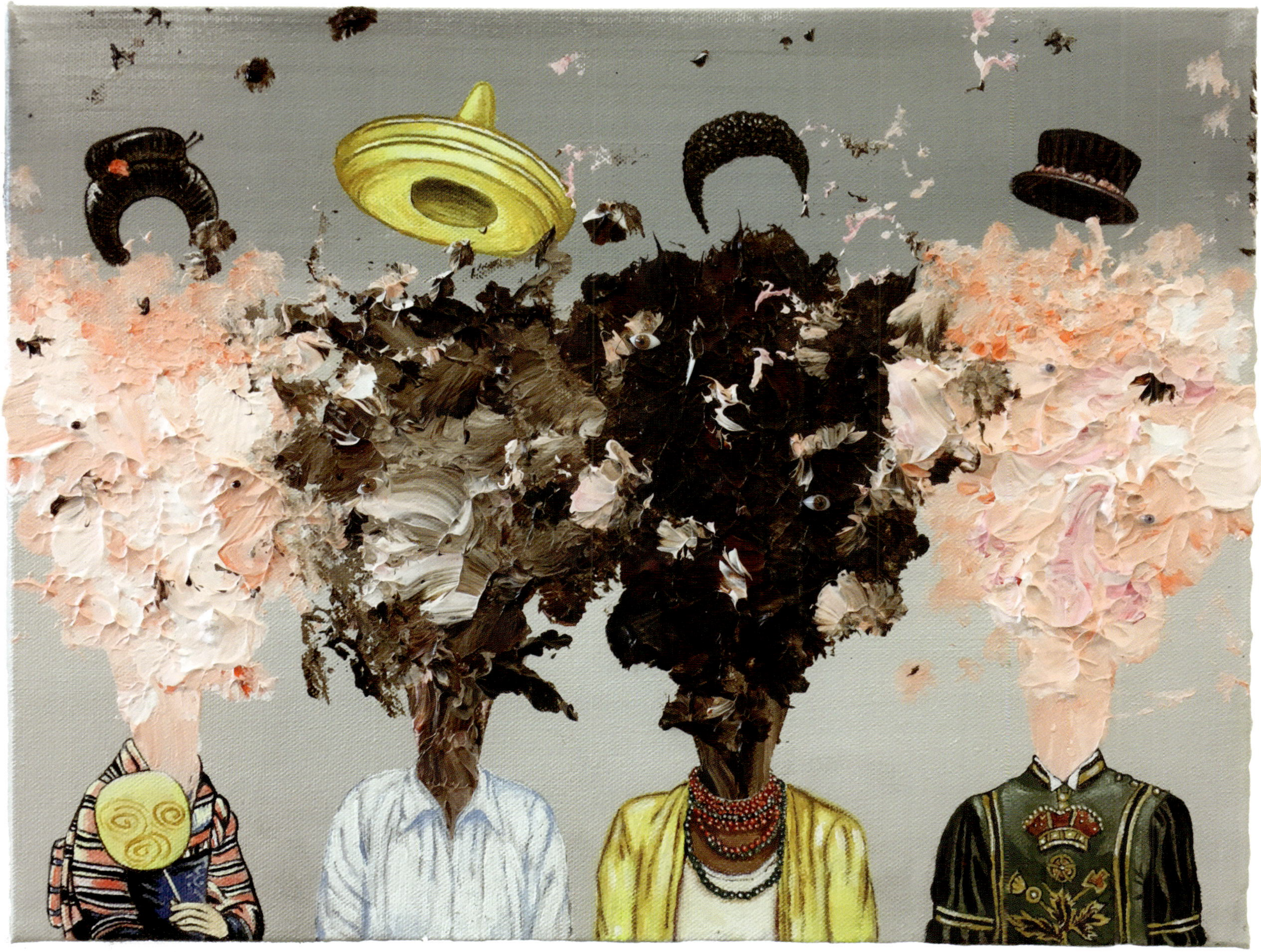

Aliens, 2018
Acrylic and water based oil on canvas, with collaged glass eye. 16 x 20 in.

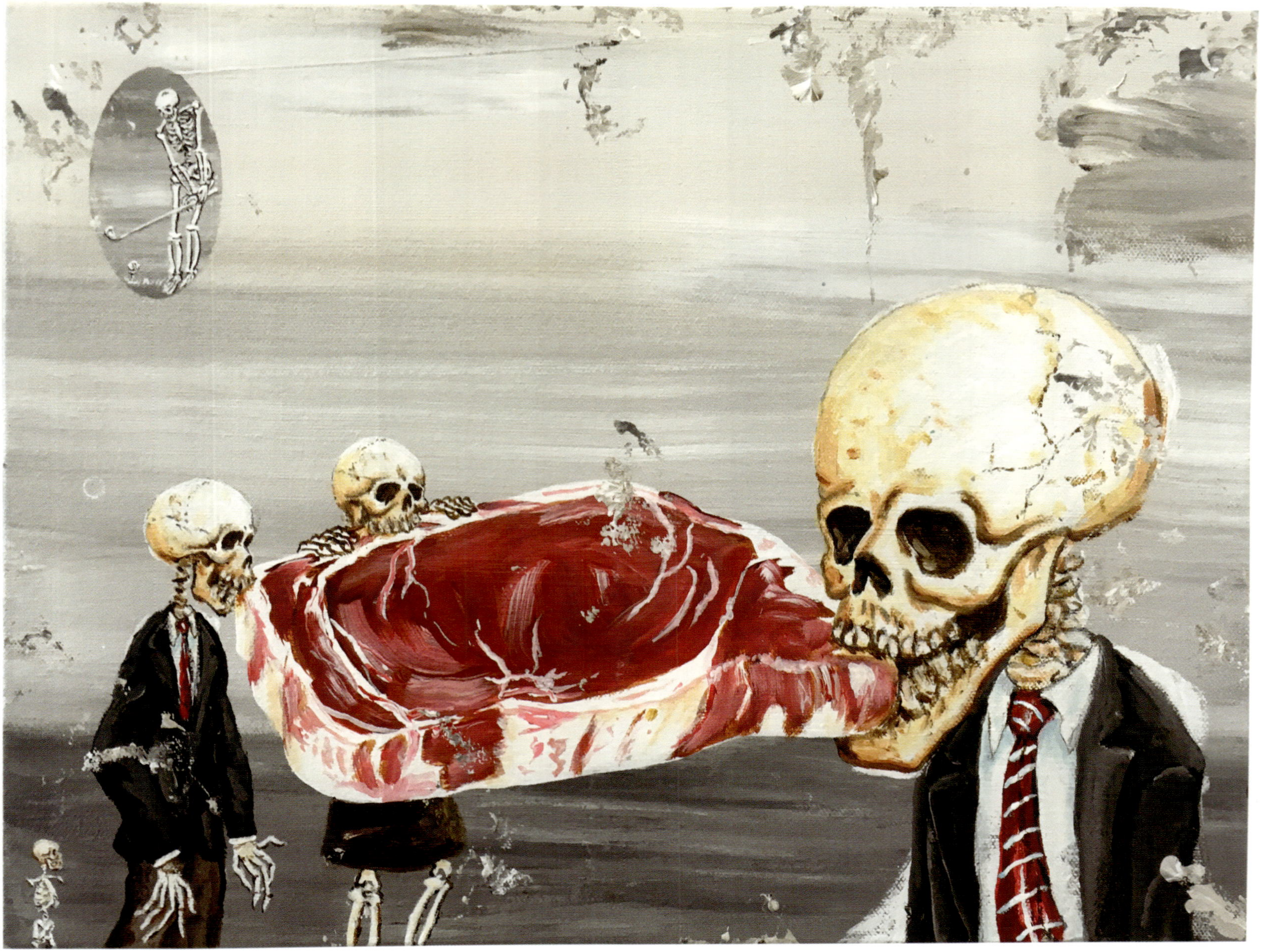

Millionaires and Billionaires, 2018
Acrylic and water based oil on canvas. 16 x 20 in.

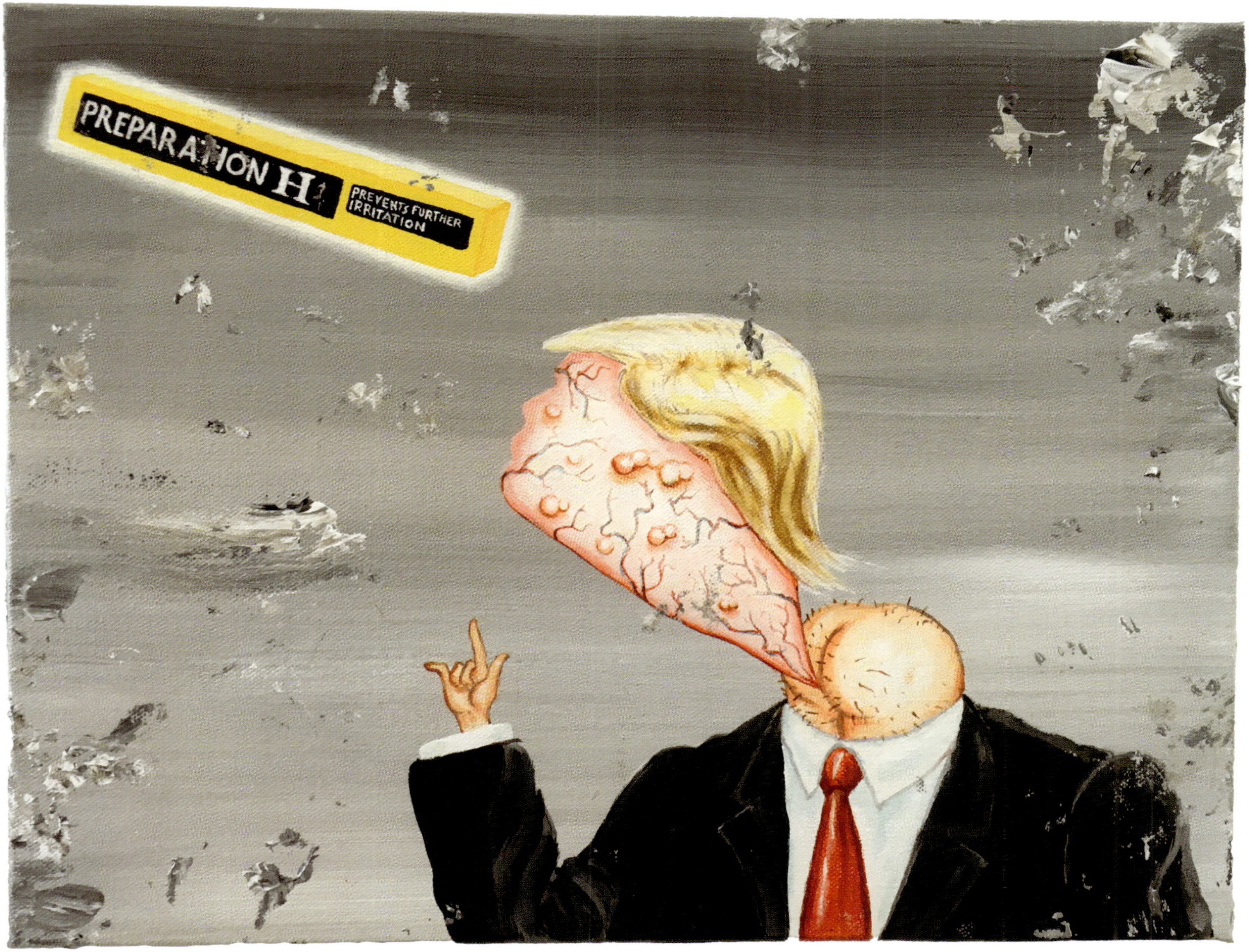

Bathroom Painting, 2018
Acrylic and water based oil on canvas. 16 x 20 in.

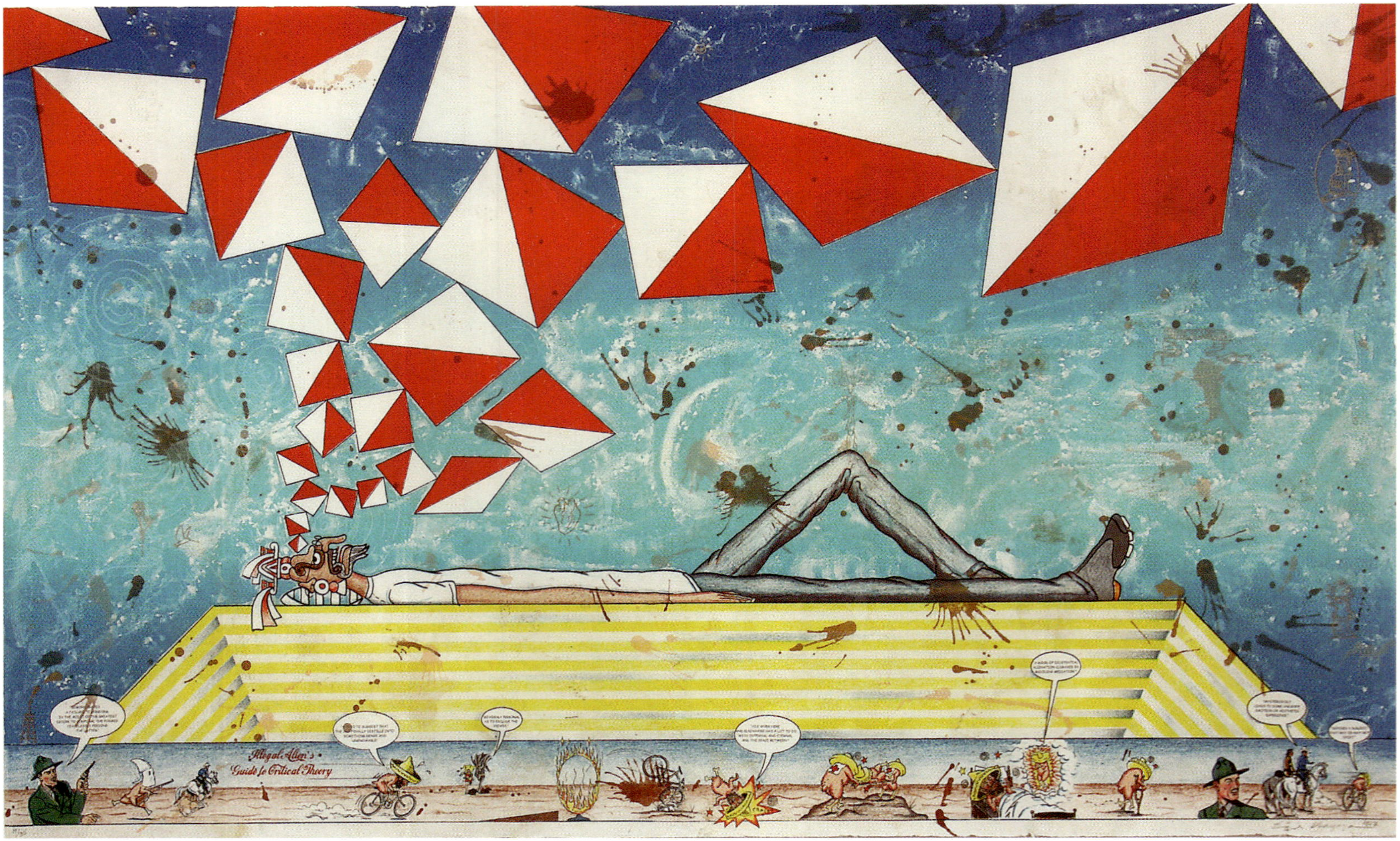

Illegal Alien's Guide to Critical Theory, 2007

Color lithograph. 24 x 40 in.

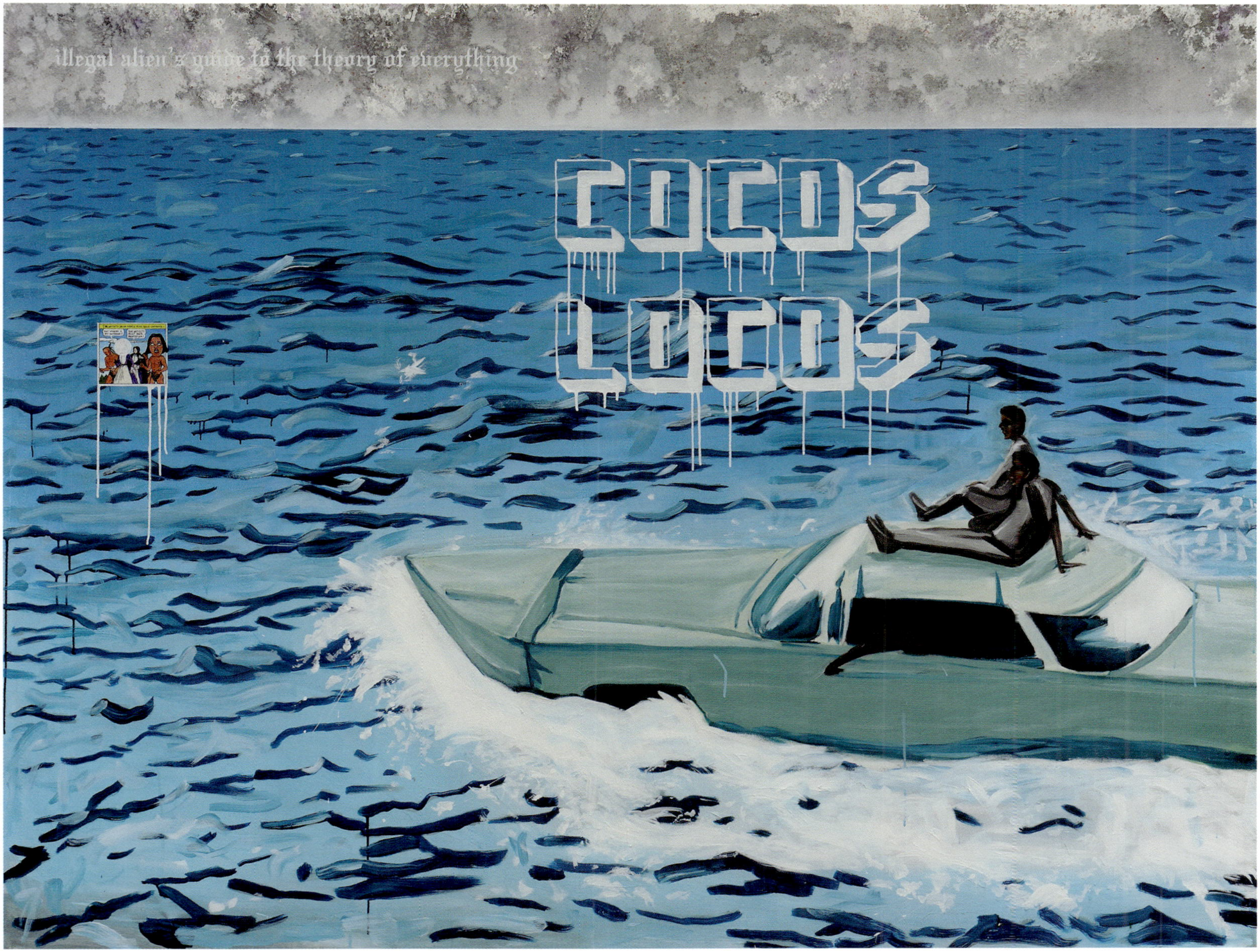

Illegal Alien's Guide to the Theory of Everything, 2006–2012
Acrylic and water based oil on canvas. 60 x 80 in.

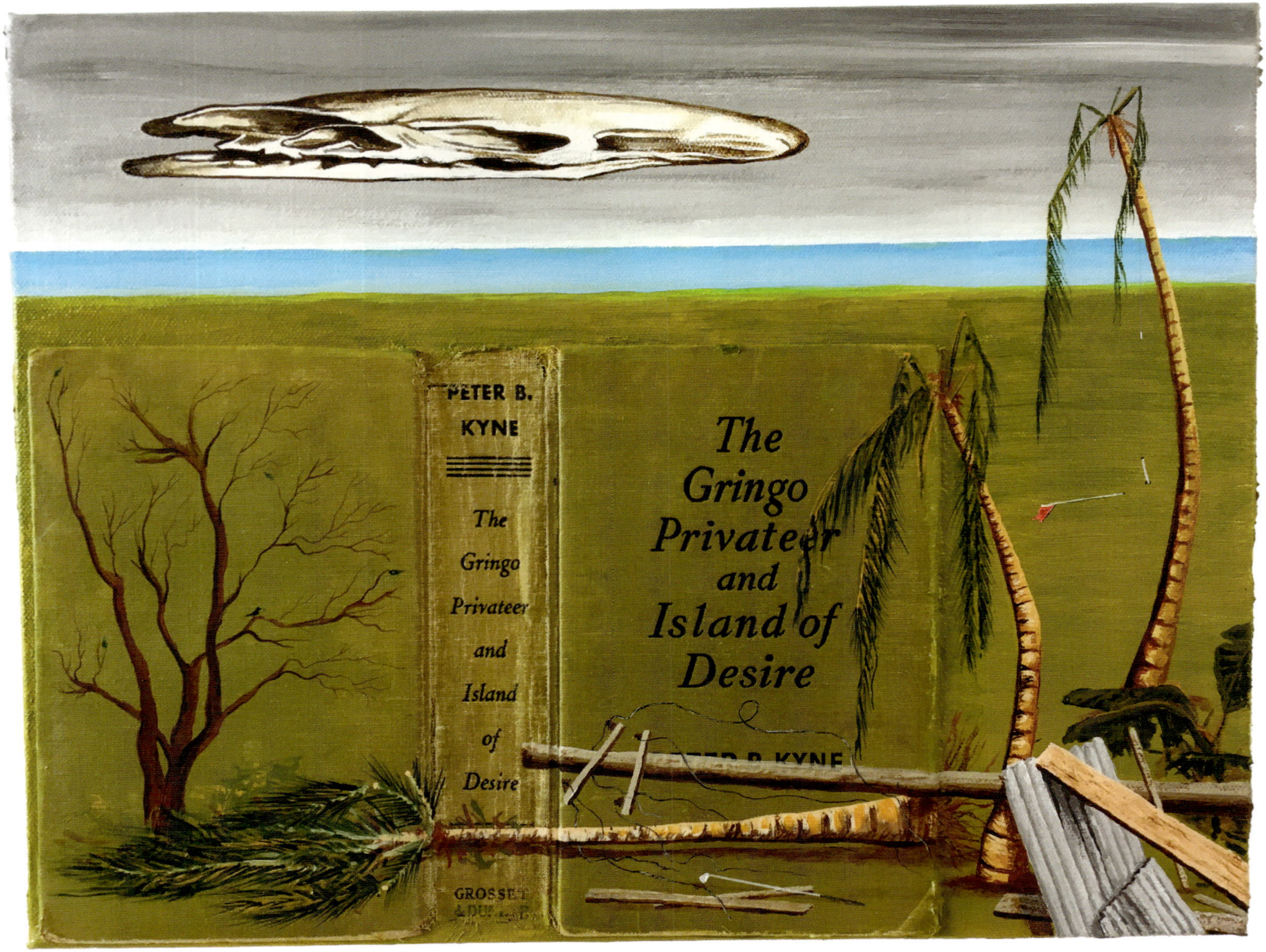

After the Hurricane, 2018

Acrylic and water based oil and collage on canvas. 16 x 20 in.

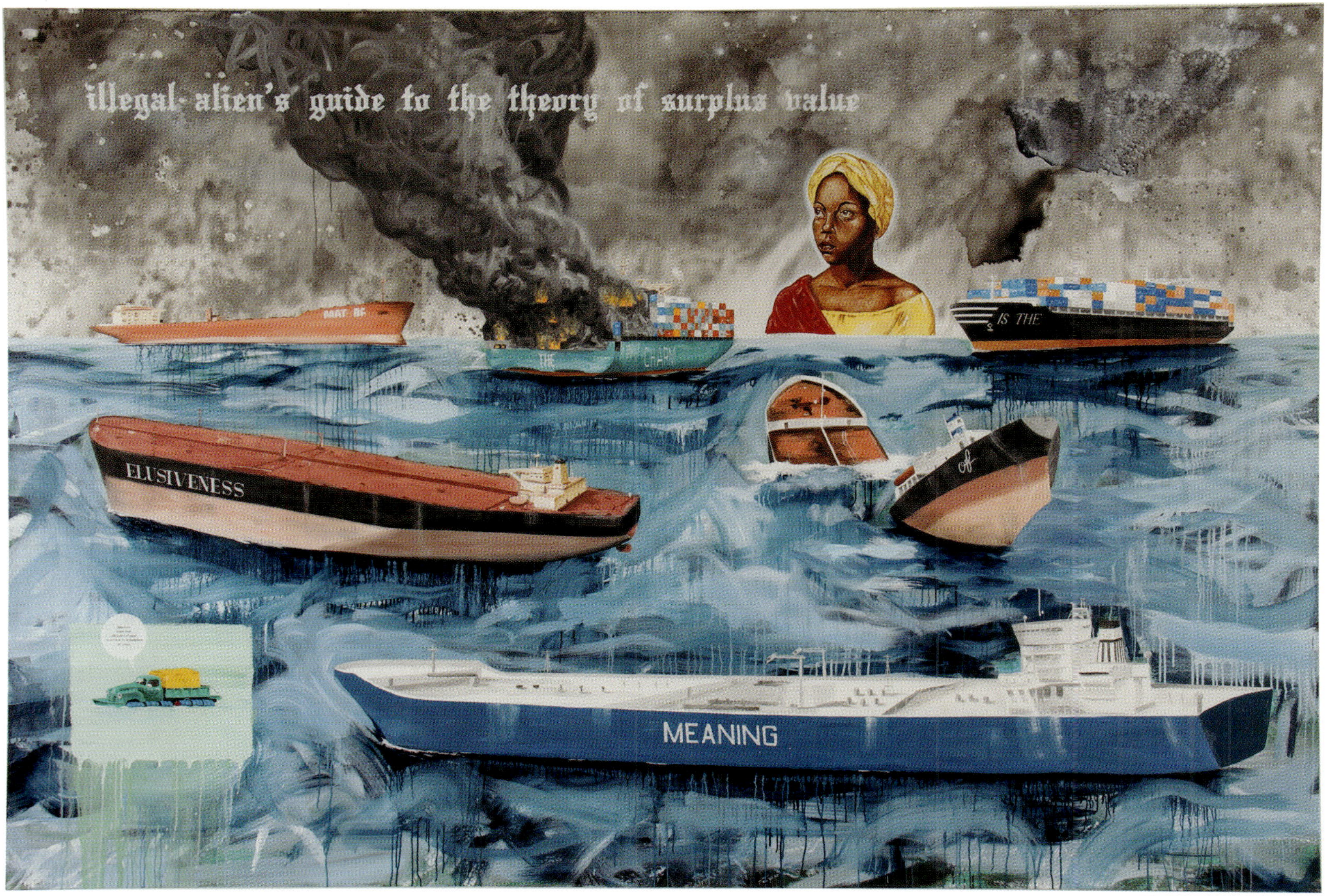

Illegal Alien's Guide to the Theory of Surplus Value, 2009
Acrylic and water based oil on canvas. 80 x 120 in.

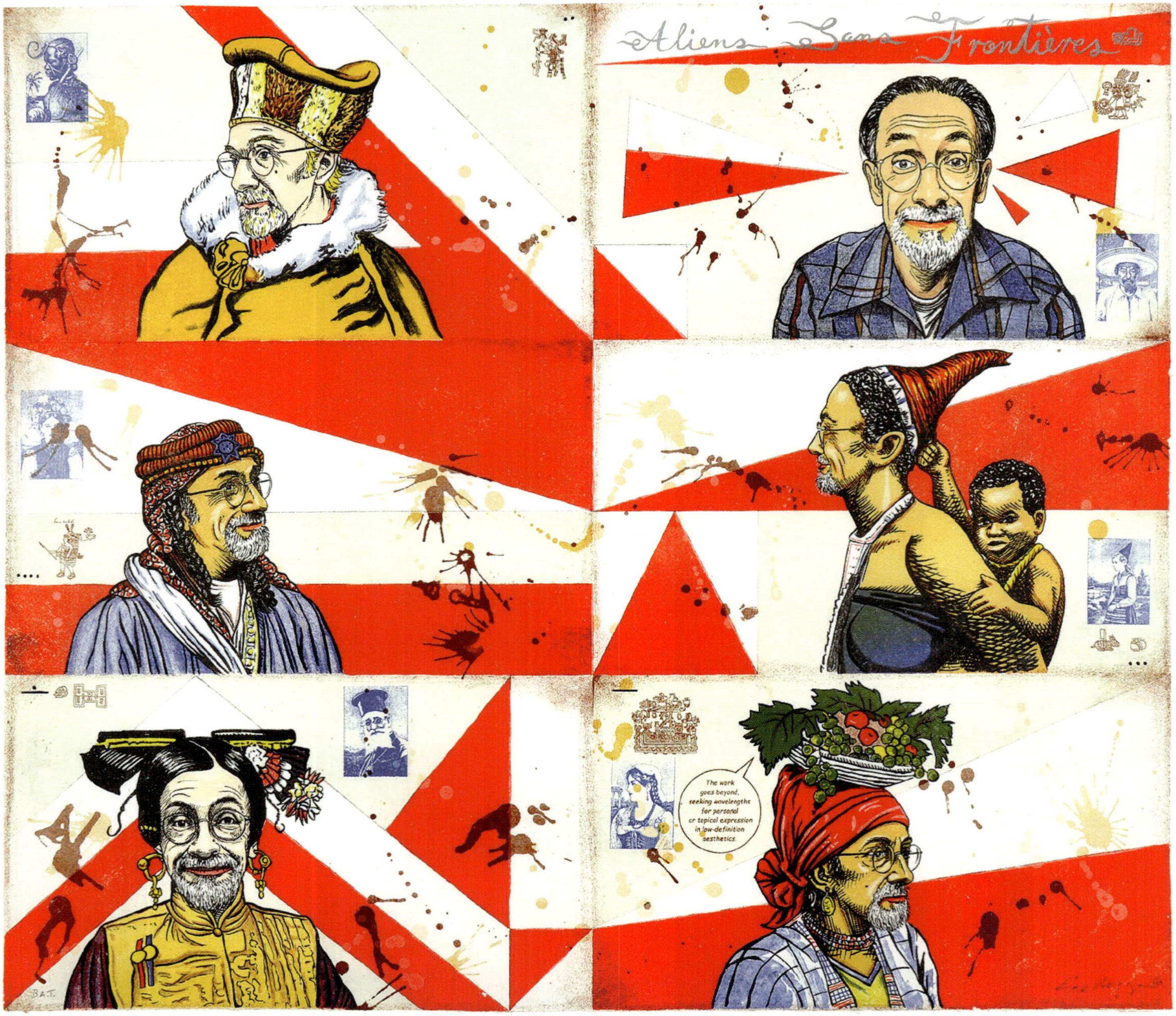

Aliens Sans Frontières, 2016

Color lithograph. 24 x 28 in.

When I made self-portraits as multiples with many ethnic representations, they were self-portraits of my DNA. I did those drawings before I got my DNA results, and they turned out to be very much like what I portrayed. My first ancestors, from 250,000 years ago, were from North Central Africa. That's where the first Chagoya was born. We are so lucky to be here alive with all these accidental mixes. We're all part of everything, a big social organism. But just as our DNA might be mixed we could have a civil war in our blood if our genes did not get along with each other. But they do get along, they make us. I think that our differences enrich our lives. The more genetic diversity we have, the better our chance for survival.

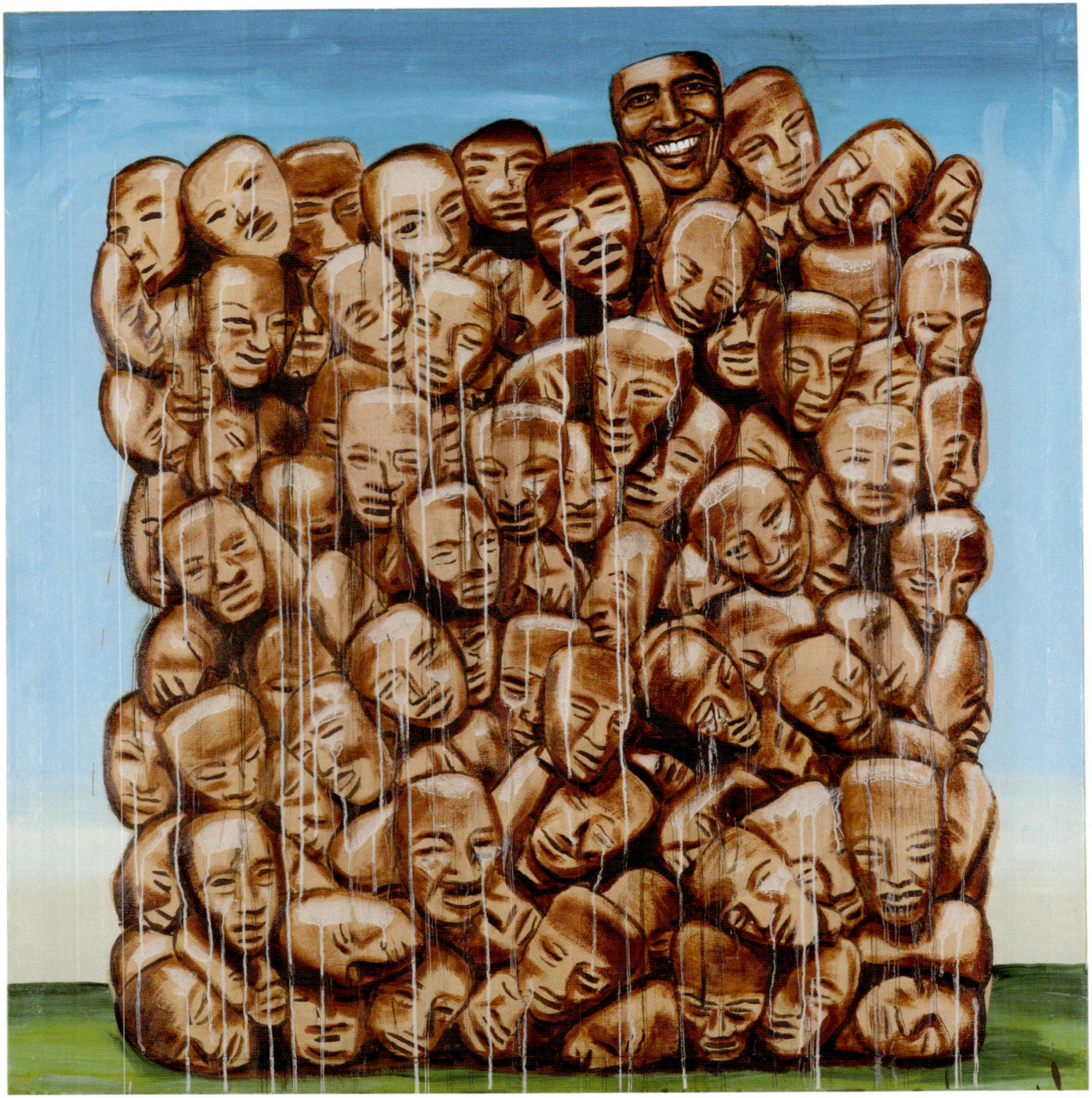

Dreamers, 2013

Acrylic and water based oil on Amate paper mounted on canvas. 48 x 48 in.

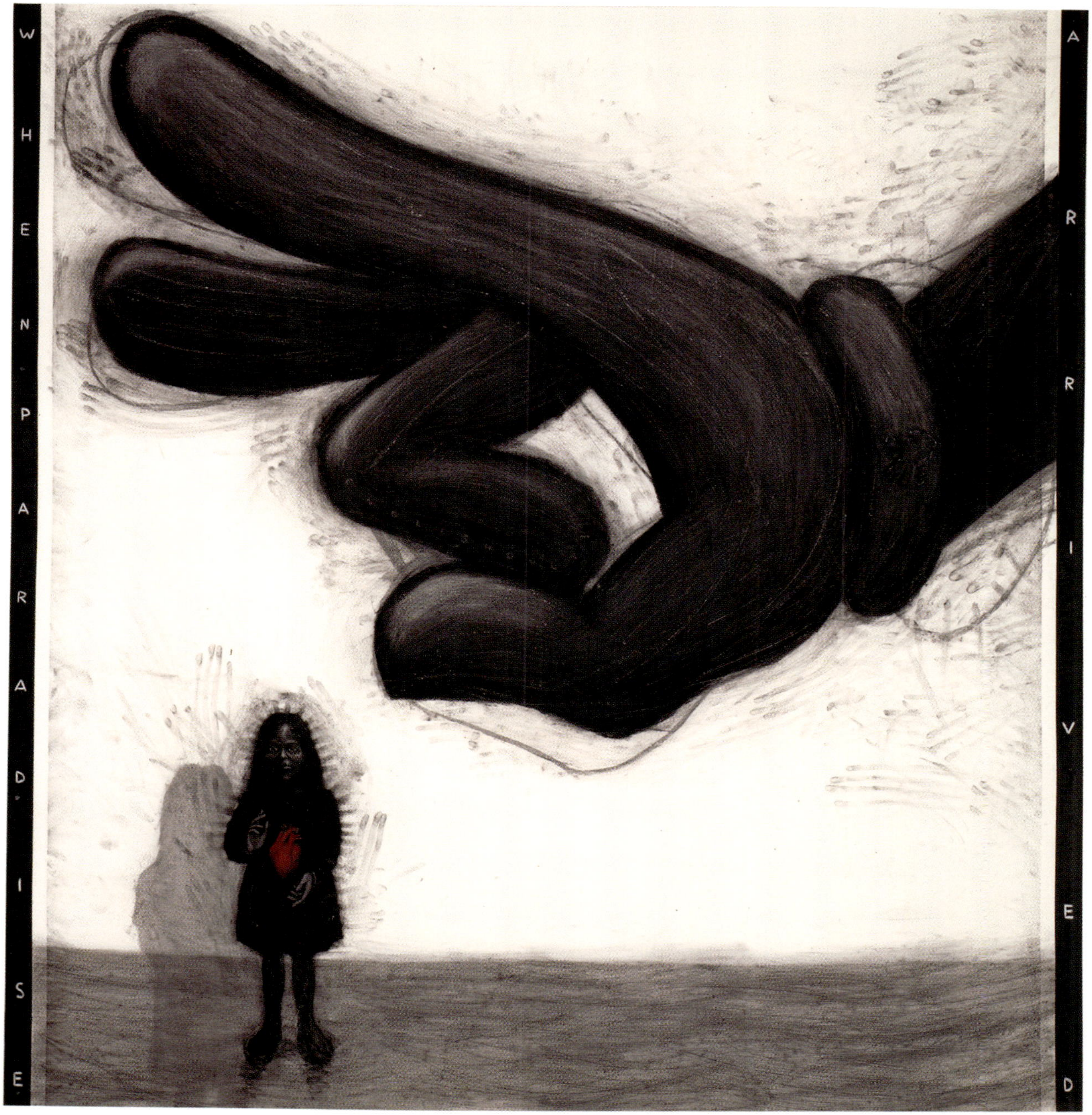

When Paradise Arrived, 1988

Charcoal and pastel on paper. 80 x 80 in.

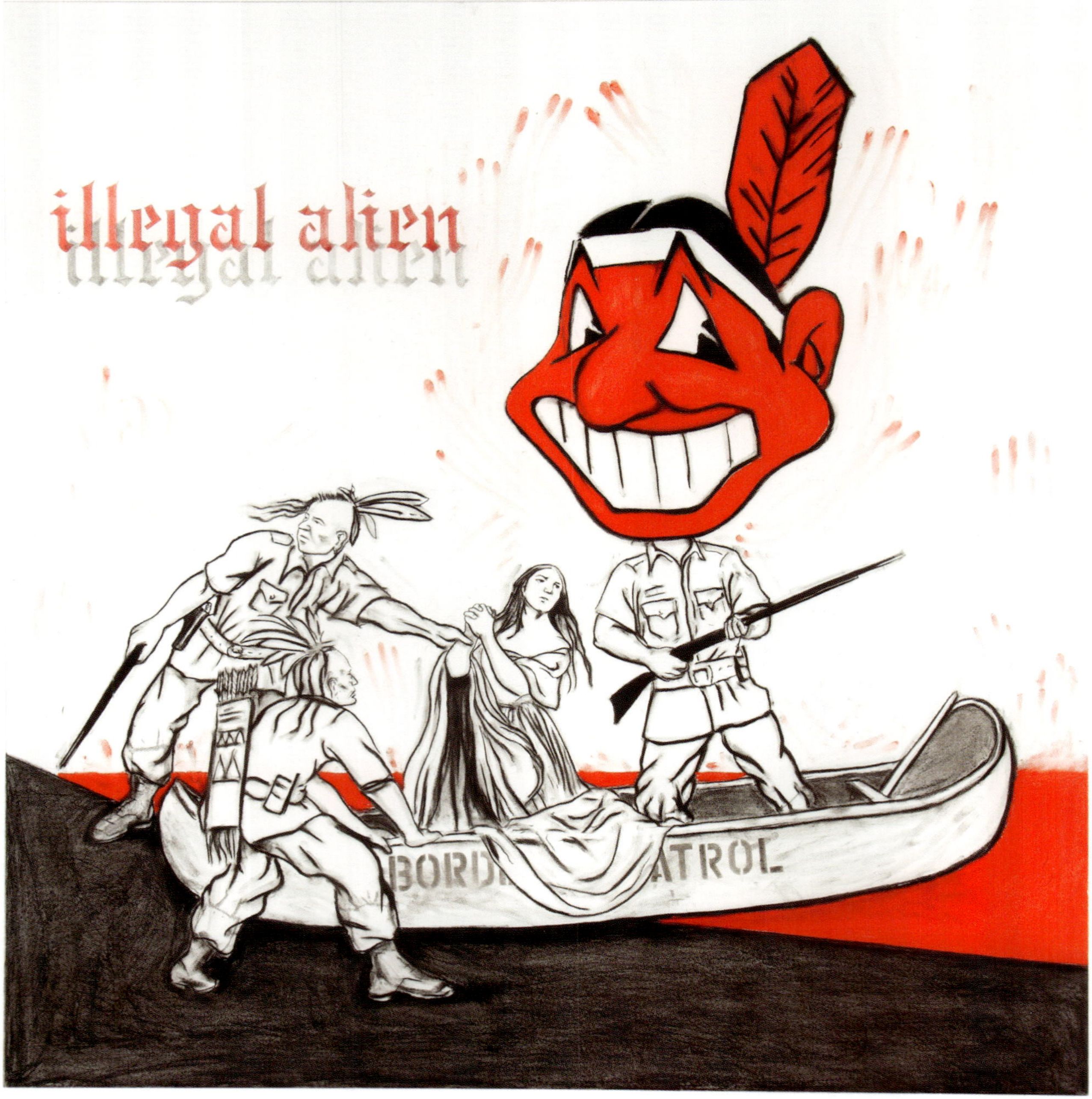

Original Border Patrol, 2006
Charcoal and pastel on paper mounted on canvas. 48 x 48 in.

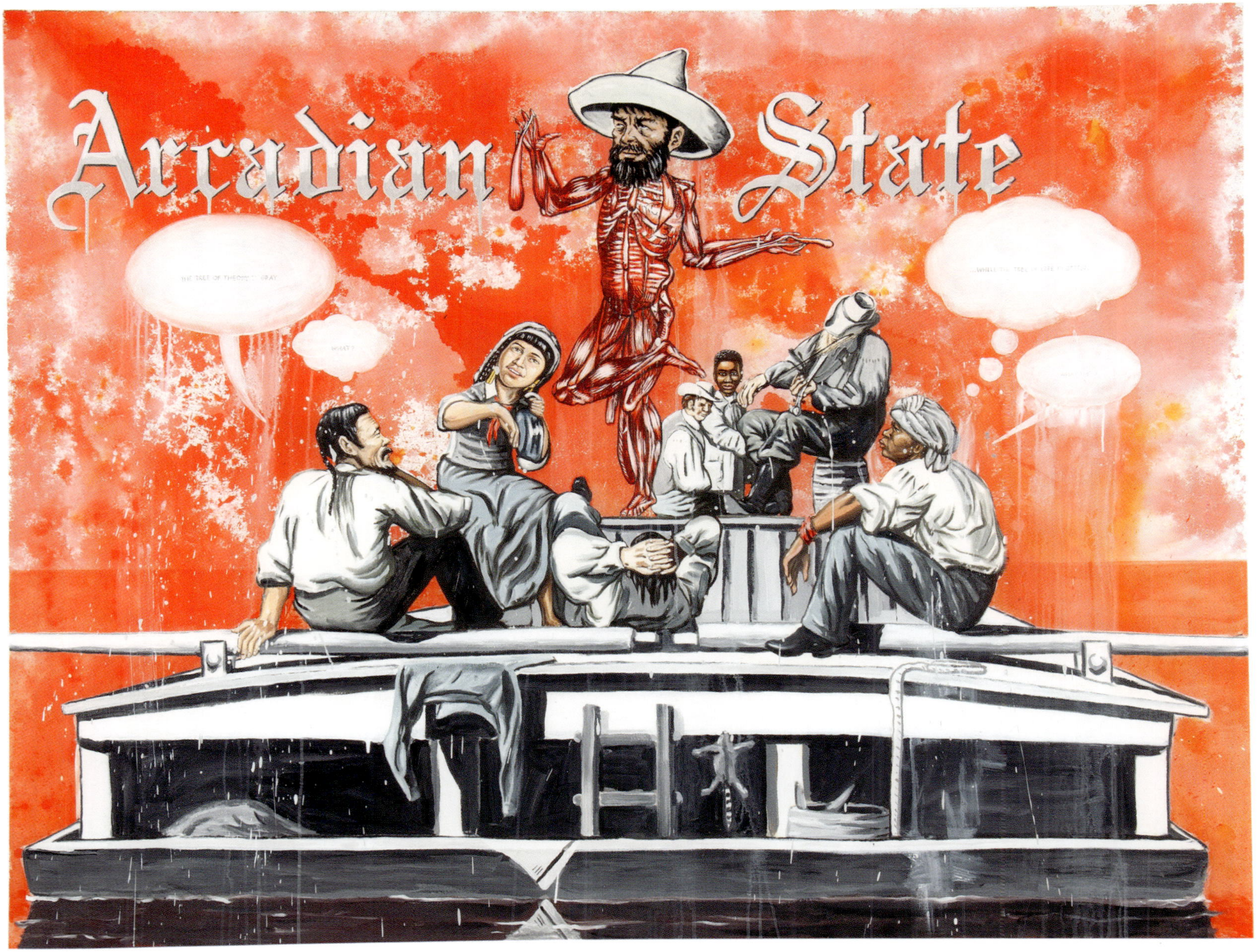

Arcadian State, 2006

Acrylic and water based oil on canvas. 60 x 80 in.

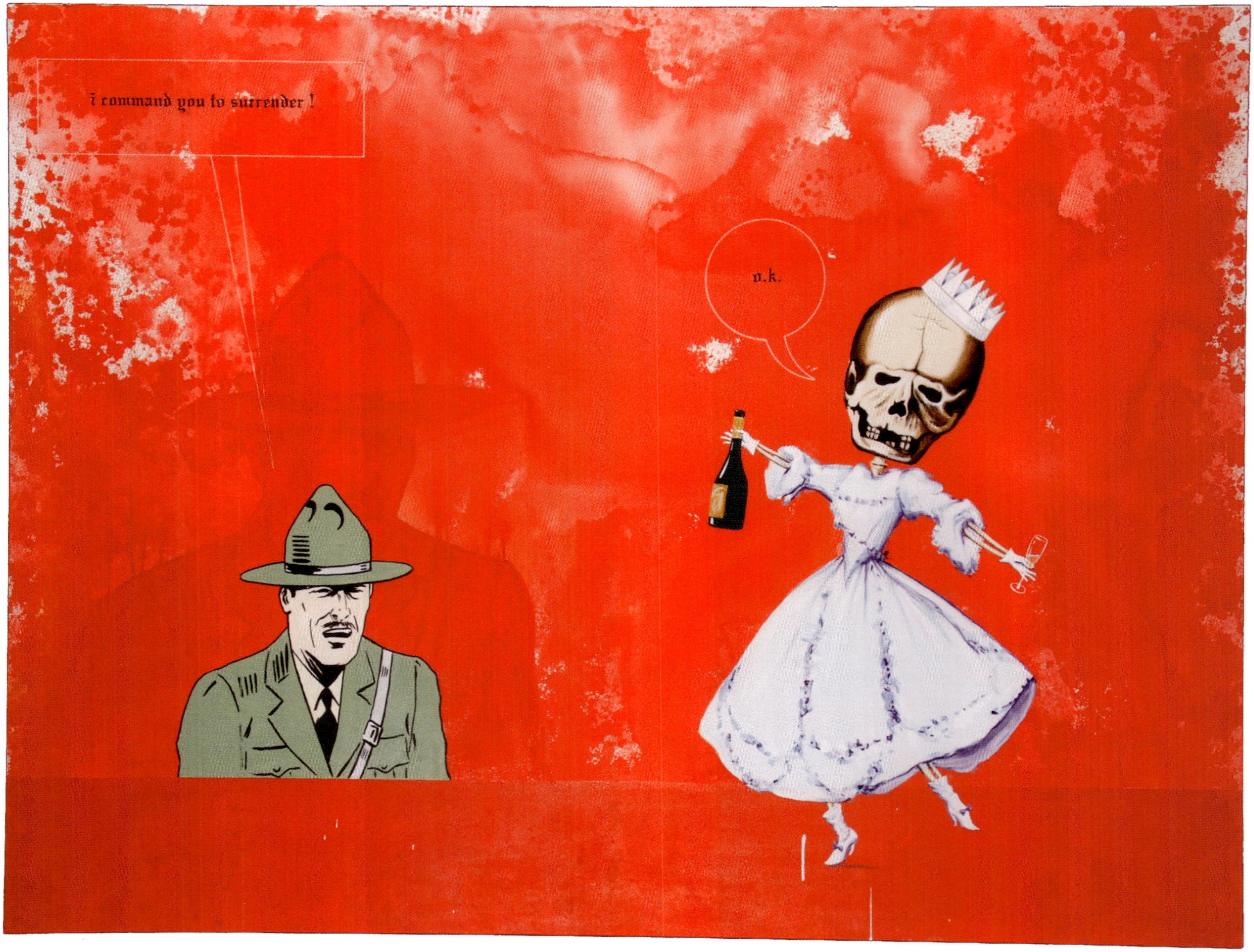

Illegal Alien's Guide to Existentialism, 2006

Acrylic and water based oil on canvas. 60 x 80 in.

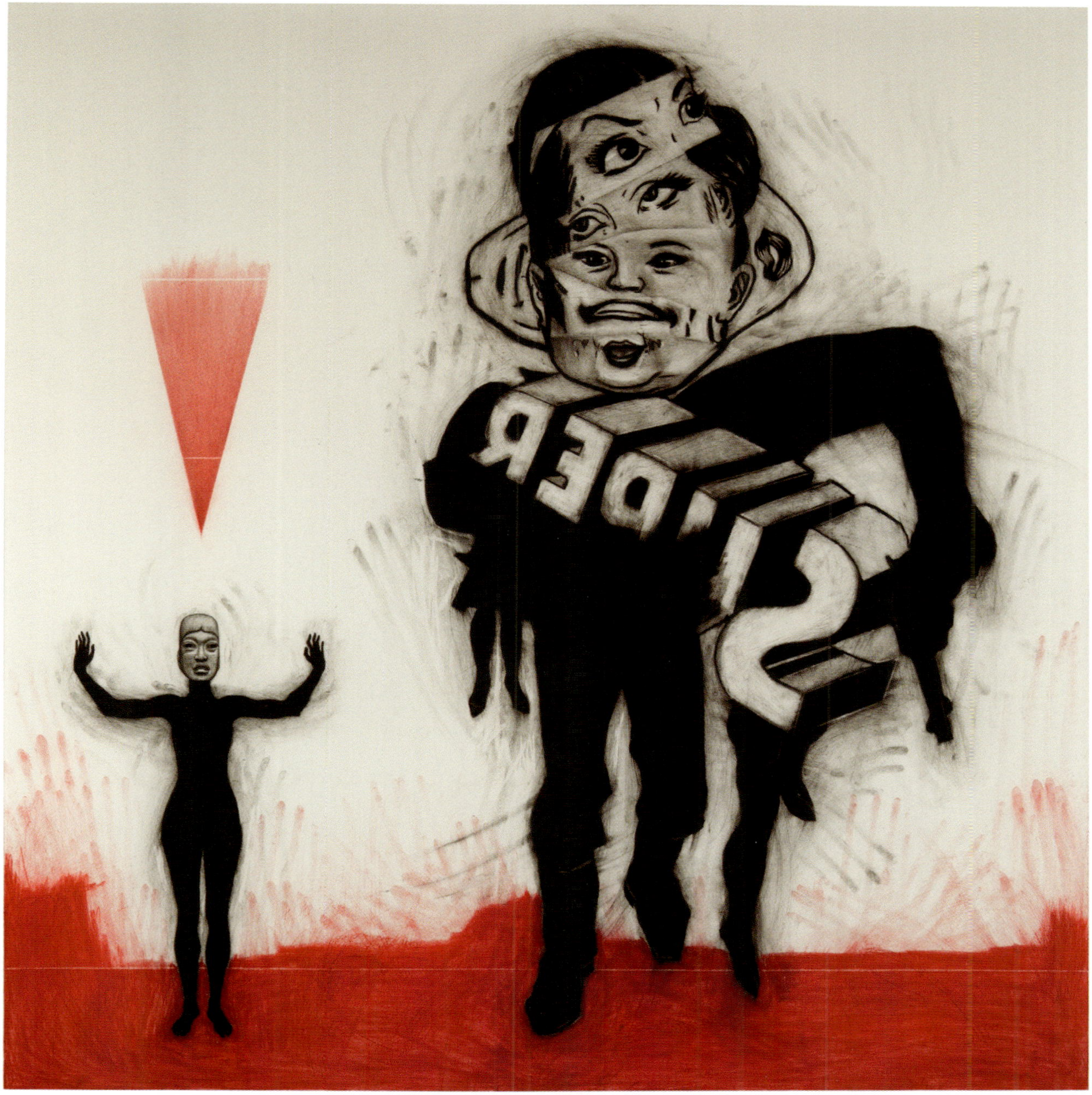

Uber Alien, 2014

Charcoal and pastel on paper mounted on canvas. 48 x 48 in.

Undocumented immigrants created this country. The first were the Spaniards, the conquistadors who went as far as Chesapeake Bay about fifty years before the Pilgrims arrived at Plymouth Rock. Then came the waves of Europeans and the slaves who were forced here from Africa. Undocumented immigrants colonized the United States and all the countries in the Americas. These colonists did not have passports because Native Americans did not issue them, but many colonizers acted against the law of the land by imposing private ownership of territories, for example. You can see that in Chief Seattle's speech, how puzzled he was that the settlers wanted to buy land and own land, whereas indigenous cultures did not own the land, but were the keepers of the land. That was the law of the land.

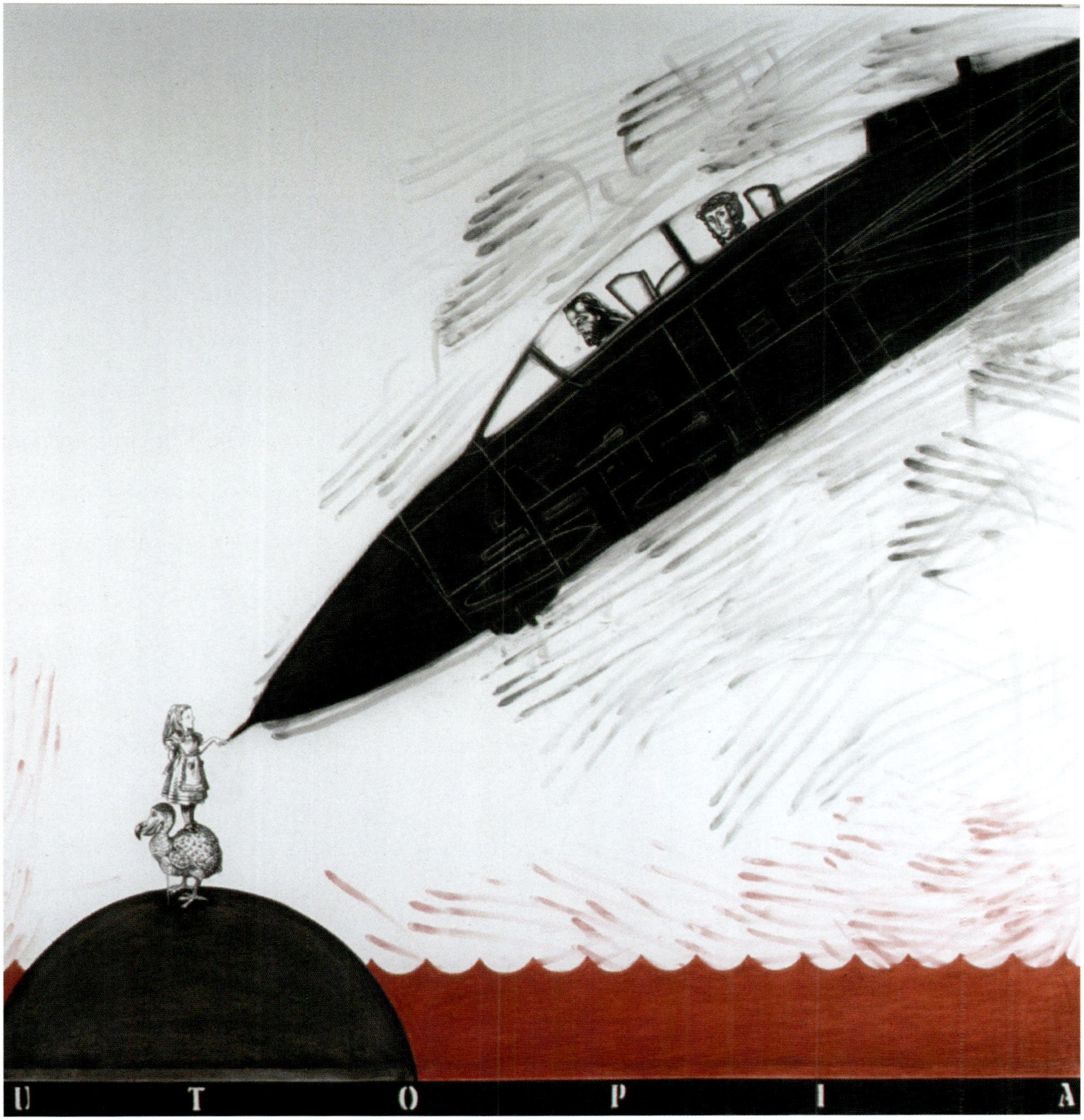

Road Map, 2006
Charcoal and pastel on paper mounted on canvas. 48 x 48 in.

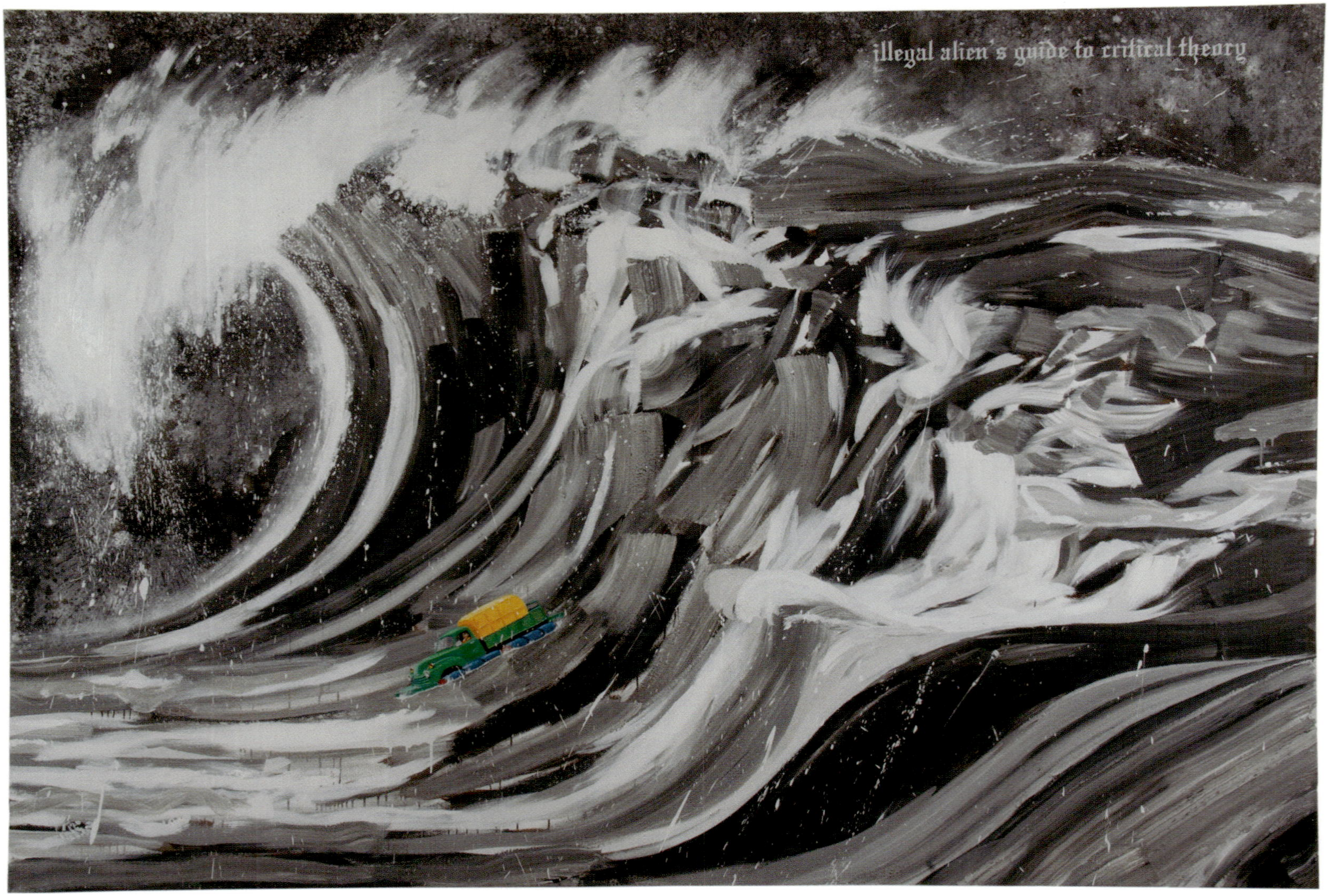

Illegal Alien's Guide to Critical Theory, 2010
Acrylic and water based oil on canvas. 80 x 120 in.

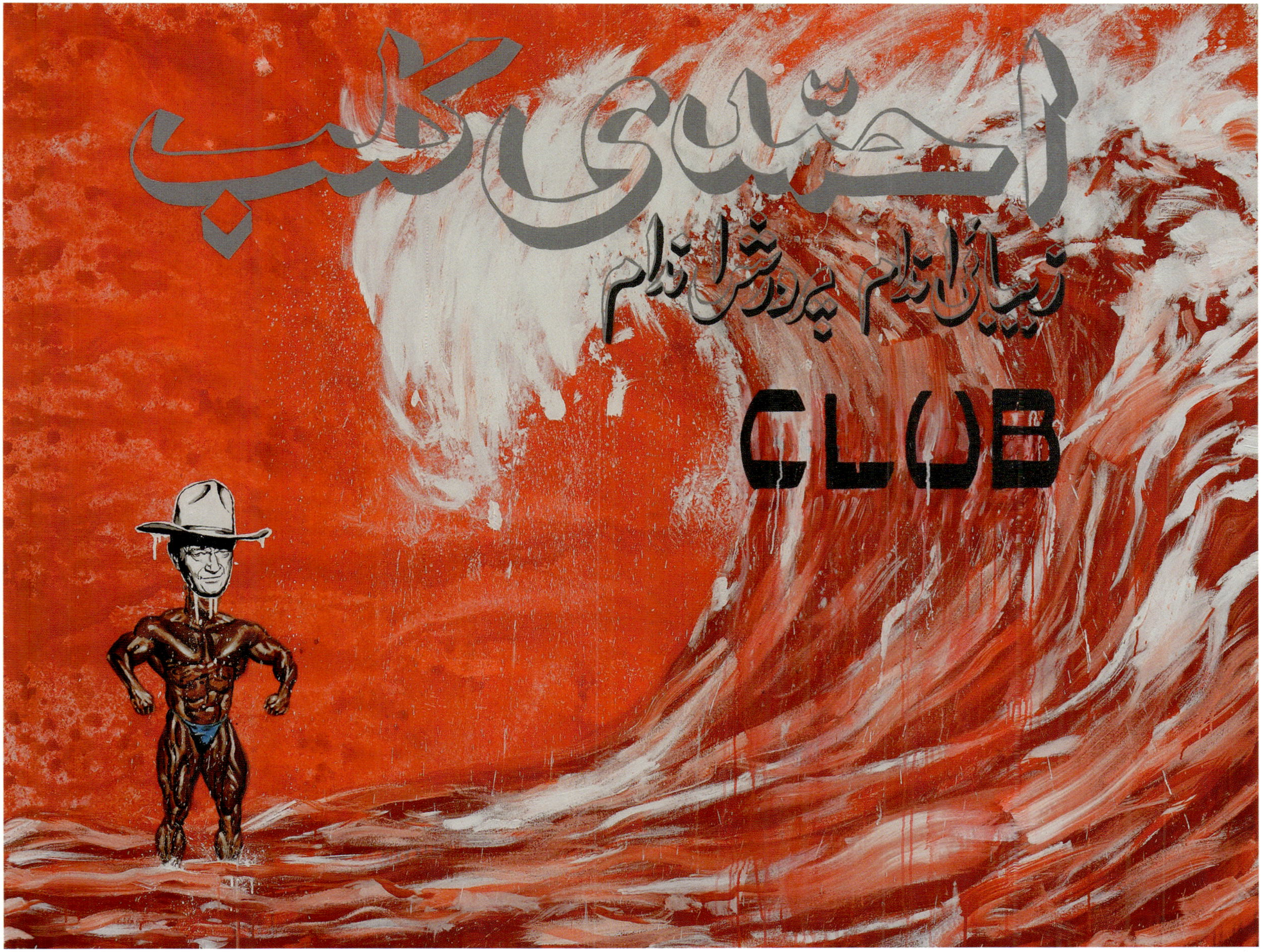

Liberty Club No. 2/Illegal Alien's Guide to Assimilation, 2006–2012
Acrylic and water based oil on canvas. 60 x 80 in.

REVERSE Anthropology

For me, reverse anthropology explores the idea that the indigenous cultures discovered Europe, not the other way around. That concept has been used by the Border Art Workshop in Tijuana and San Diego. Beginning in the mid-eighties some members of the Border Art Workshop developed the fantasy that the Aztecs arrived in Europe and began to build pyramids and destroy the cathedrals, things like that. So I understand that perspective, but my focus is more on my codices and appropriations of European art, rather than on conquering other cultures, which renders everybody in the same box.

I briefly studied anthropology in Mexico City. The history of anthropology is interesting. It originated in England as a need for the English to better understand their colonies. Eventually it became the progressive science it is today. People claim that the first anthropologist was Fray Bernardino de Sahagún, who compiled the history of the Aztecs in a 2,400-page codex, organized in twelve volumes, known as the Codex Florentino. This happened after the destruction of most pre-Columbian books during the conquest war. In my work with reverse anthropology, I explore what would happen if an indigenous artist took over European books. In the 1990s I began to paint over books and 19th century prints by European artists that I found in the flea market, getting moldy and semi-destroyed, and gave them a new life with pre-Columbian imagery.

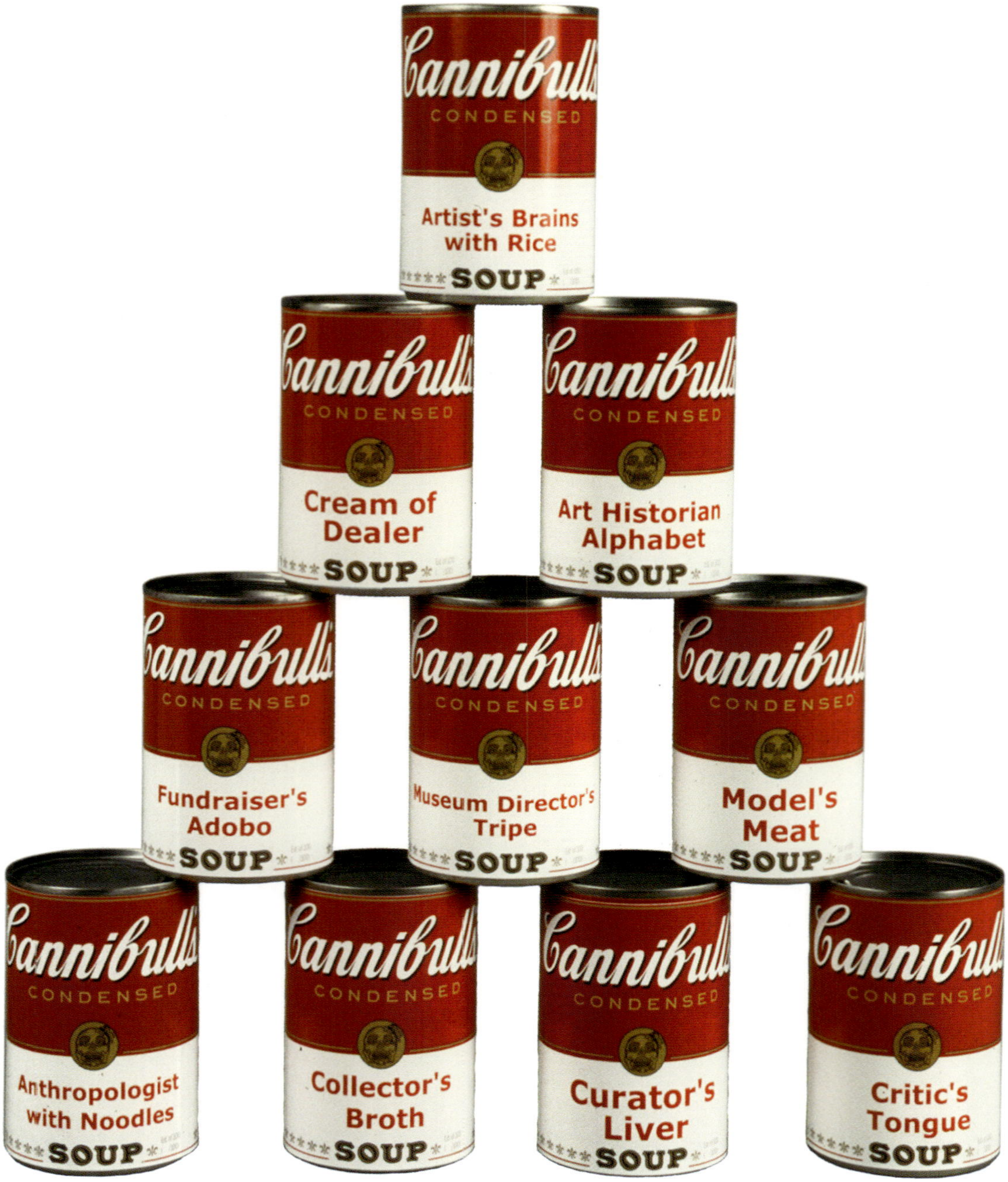

The Enlightened Savage, 2002

Ten tin cans with digital labels and filled with silica sand. 4 x 2 1/2 in. each

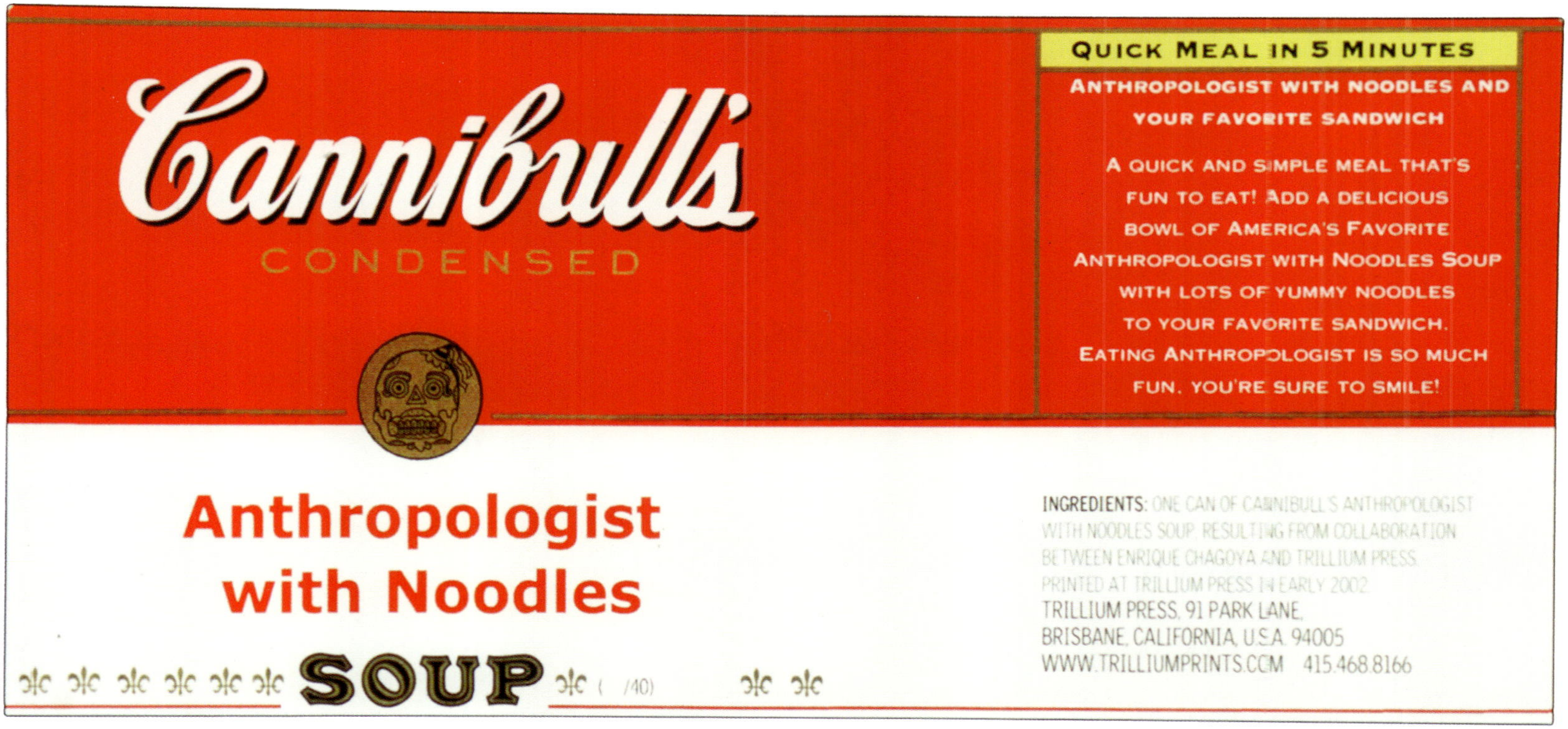

The Enlightened Savage, 2002
Detail (can label)

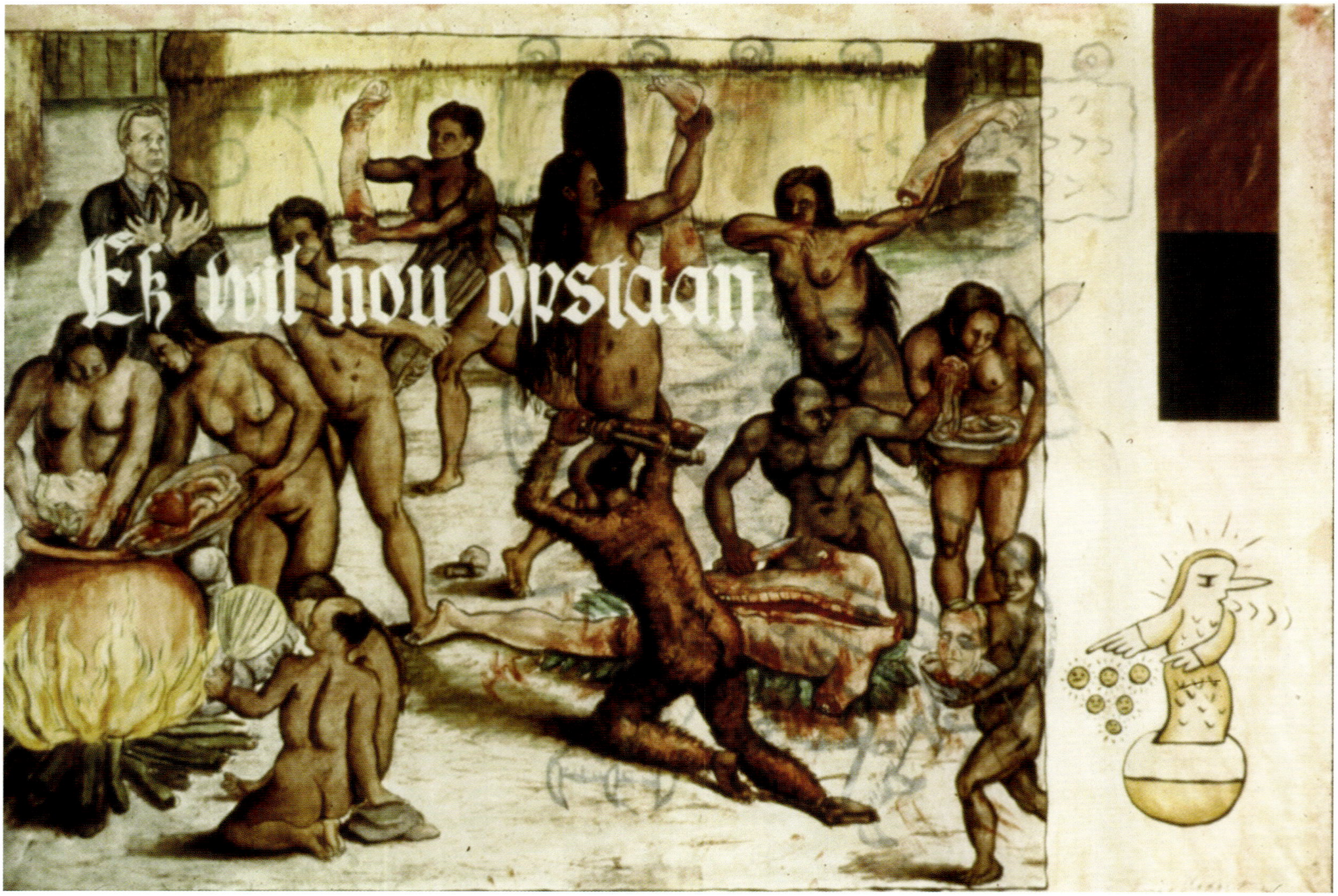

Xenophobic Nightmare in a Foreign Language, 1994

Acrylic and water based oil on Amate paper. 48 x 60 in.

Words in Afrikaans translate as "I want to wake up now."

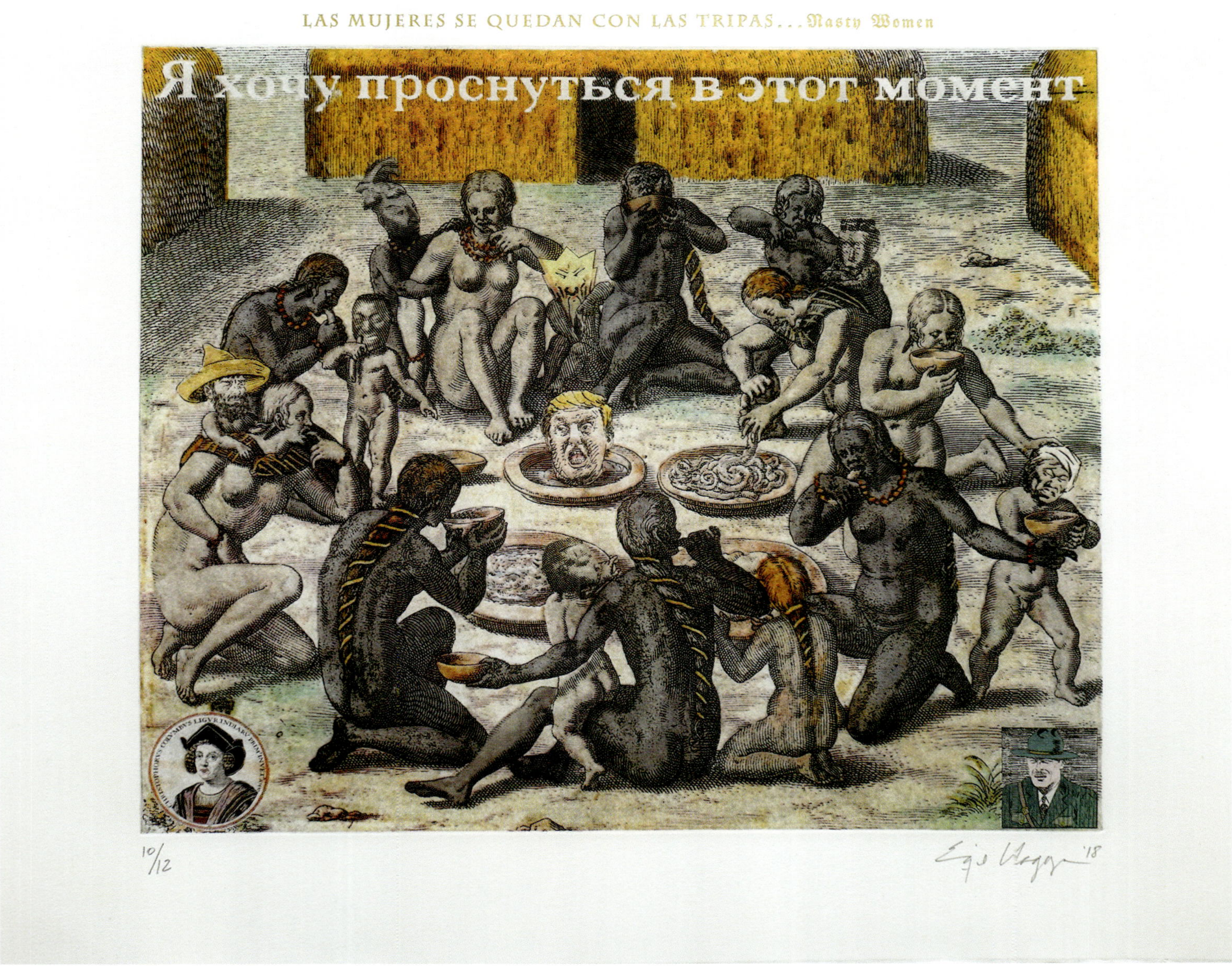

The President's Xenophobic Nightmare in a Foreign Language, 2018

Etching on copper with letterpress stamp and digitally printed colors. 22 x 25 1/4 in.

Words in Russian translate as "I want to wake up at this moment." In Spanish as "The woman kept the tripes."

By the time I grew up in Mexico City there'd been a long history of satirical cartooning, a couple of hundred years. It especially flourished during the revolution. Graphic artists like José Guadalupe Posada (1852-1913) became popular for making fun of people during the Day of the Dead, drawing cartoons of living people as skeletons, with poems that described their fictitious deaths. Today it would be like making a cartoon of Donald Trump as a skeleton with a funny poem about how he died in Russia with Putin. When I grew up right after the student movement in 1968, with a lot of political changes and turmoil in the country, many artists turned to cartooning and political satire.

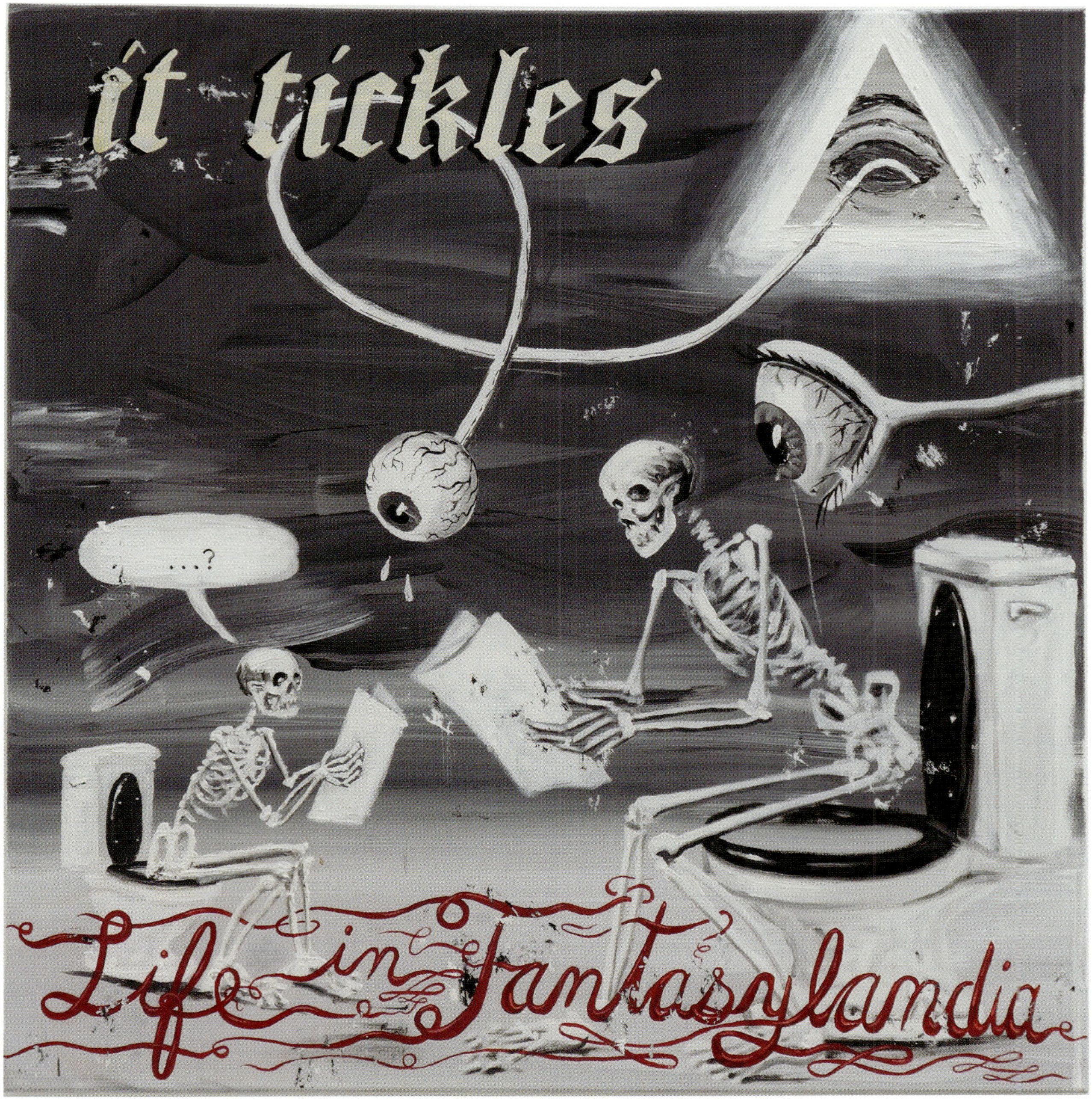

Life in Fantasylandia, 2013–2016
Acrylic on canvas. 30 x 30 in.

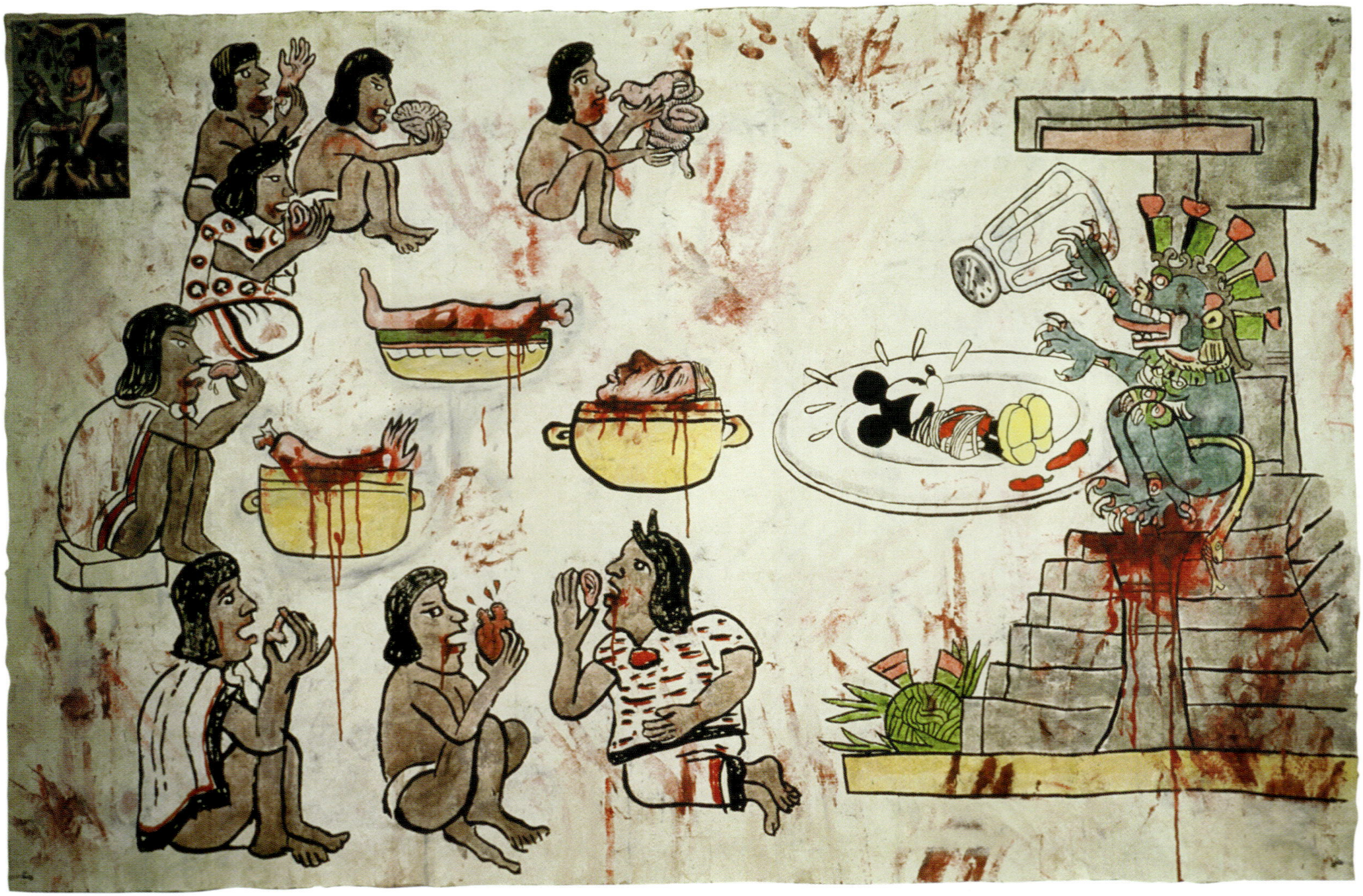

The Governor's Nightmare, 1994
Acrylic and water based oil on Amate paper. 48 x 60 in.

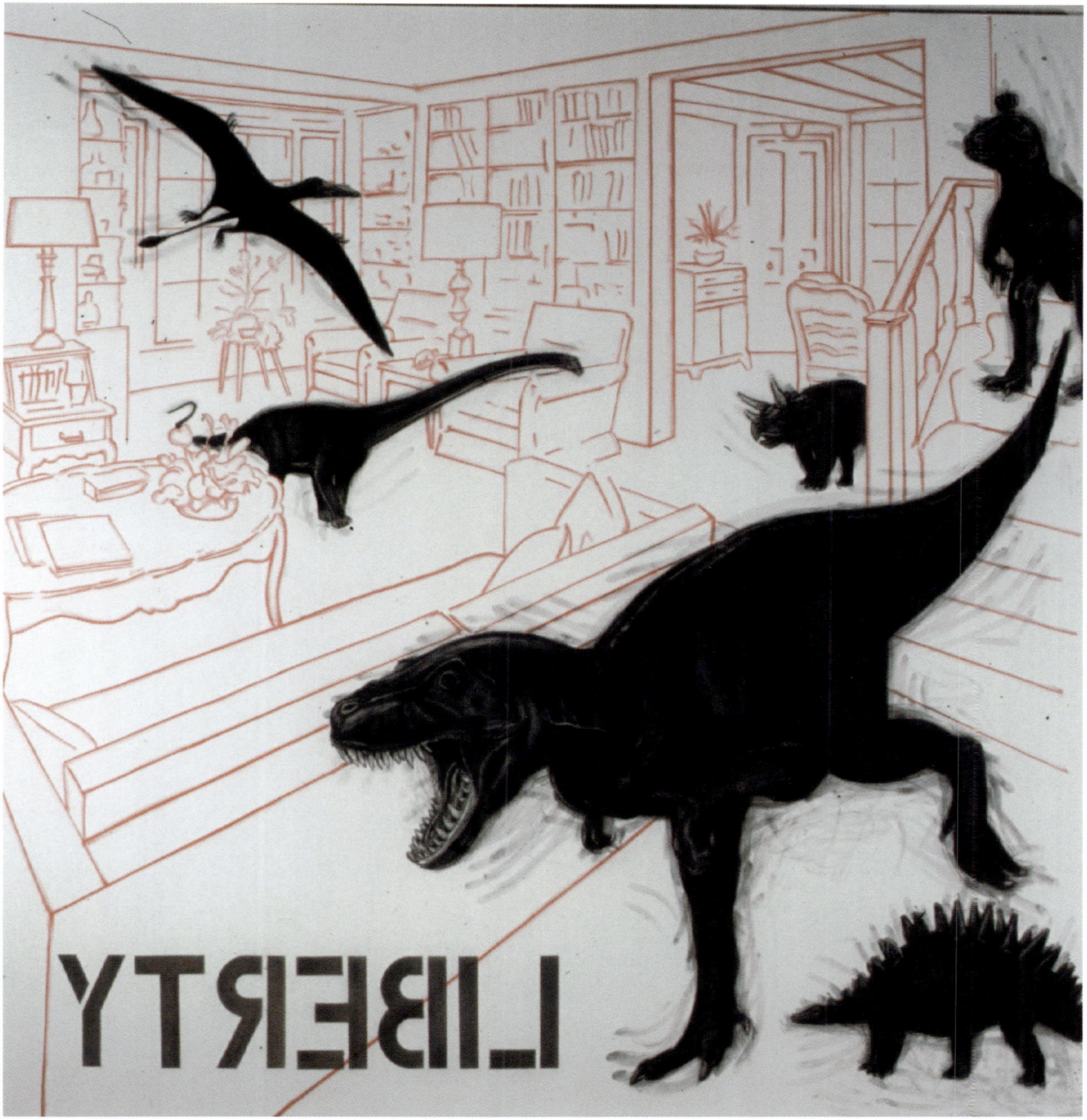

Liberty, 2006

Charcoal and pastel on paper mounted on canvas. 48 x 48 in.

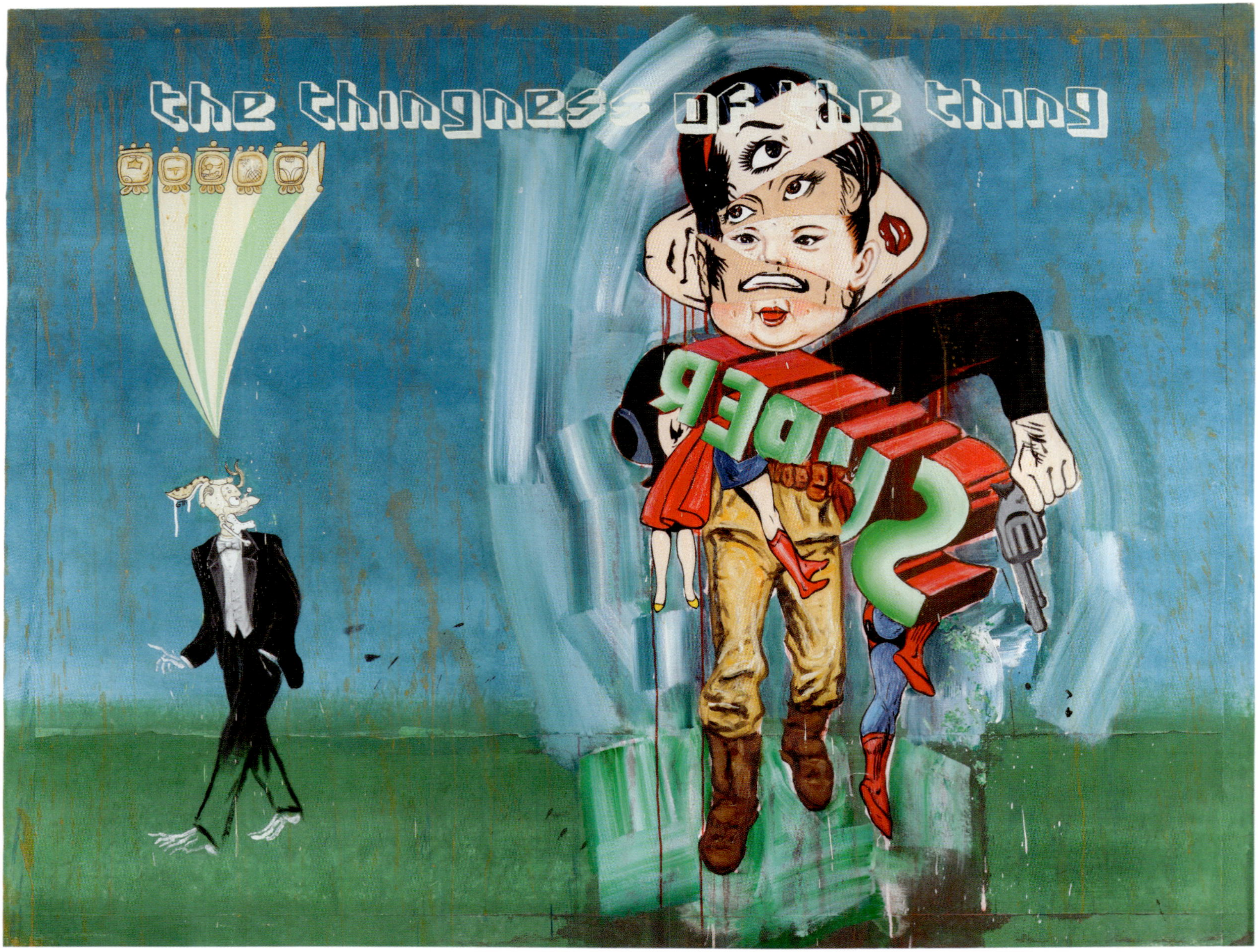

The Ongoing Escape from Fantasylandia, 2013

Acrylic and water based oil on Amate paper mounted on canvas. 60 x 80 in.

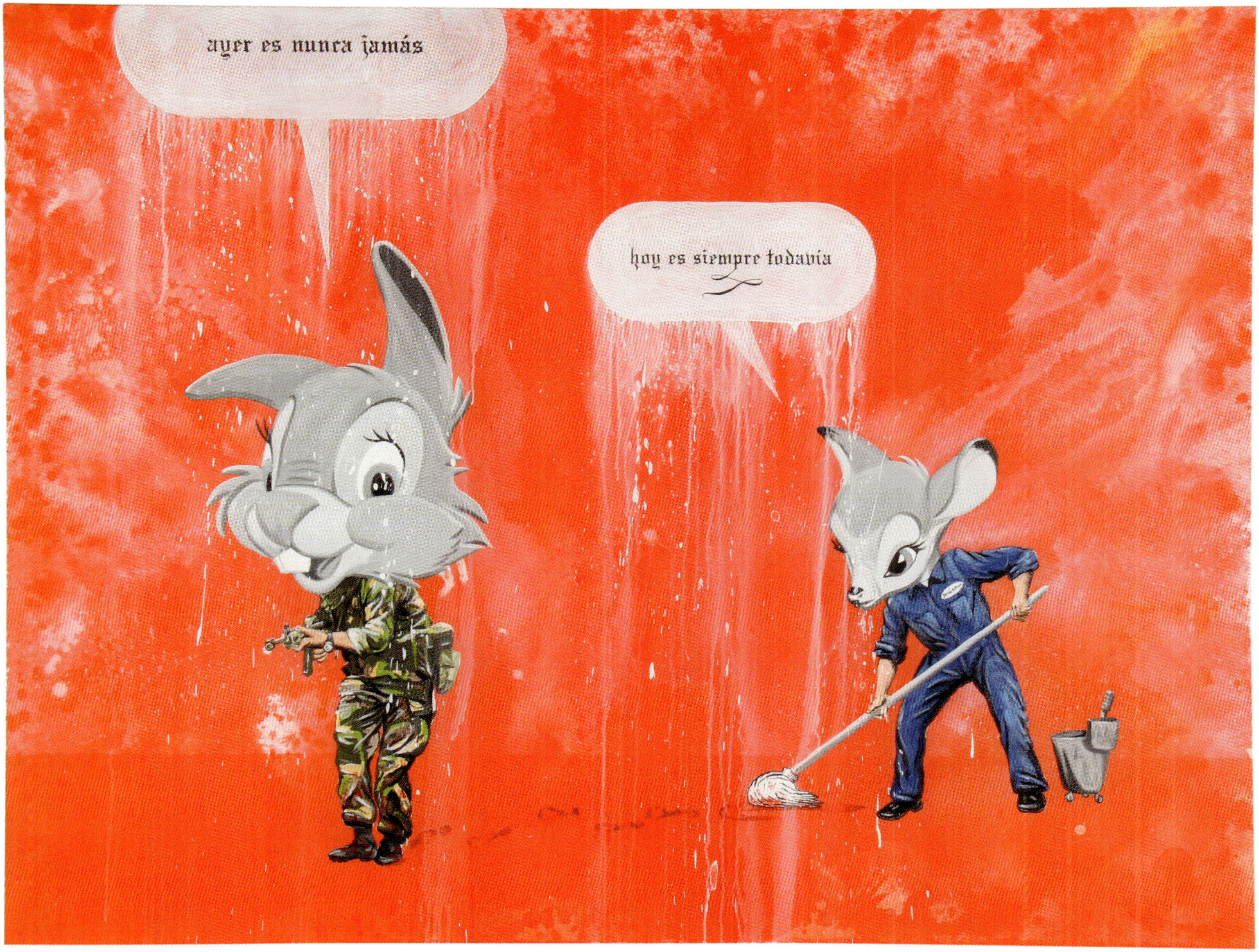

Yesterday is Never Again/Today is Still Forever, 2006
Acrylic and water based oil on canvas. 60 x 80 in.

Humor plays a large part in Mexican culture. There are always jokes about tragedies that happen in the country, something that I don't see anywhere else in the world. I think Mexican humor has its roots in pre-Columbian cultures. They had a different idea of death in which life was seen as a dream. In anonymous pre-Columbian poems from the Aztecs, from the Nahuatl culture, there is a saying, life is a dream and then you wake up. For the Aztecs life was really a dream and when you died your life began as a dead person, and there was a celebration because that person was beginning a new life.

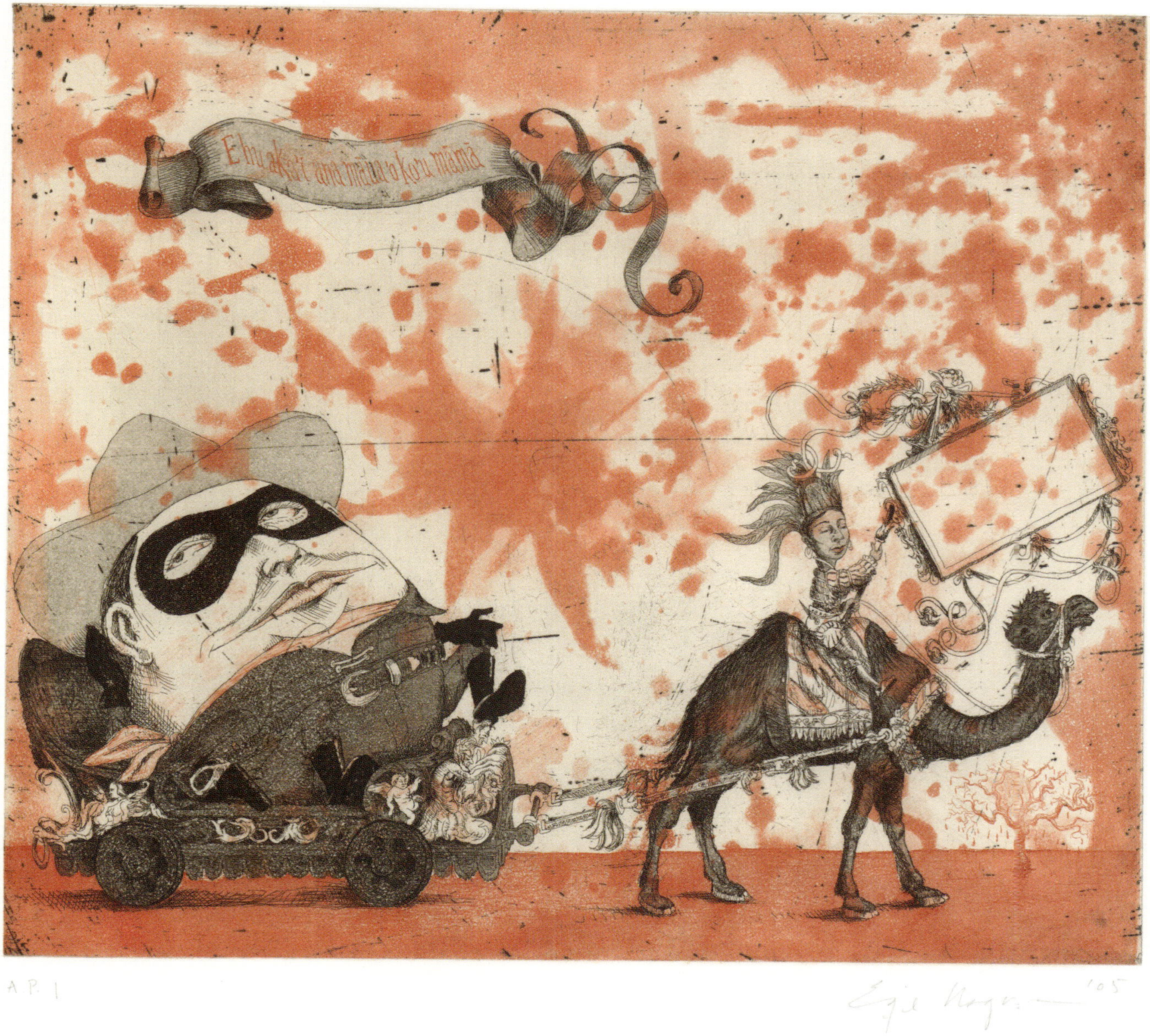

Liberty on the Road, 2005

Etching on copper. 24 x 35 in.

Words in Hawaiian on banner translate as "Mom and I are going on a holiday."

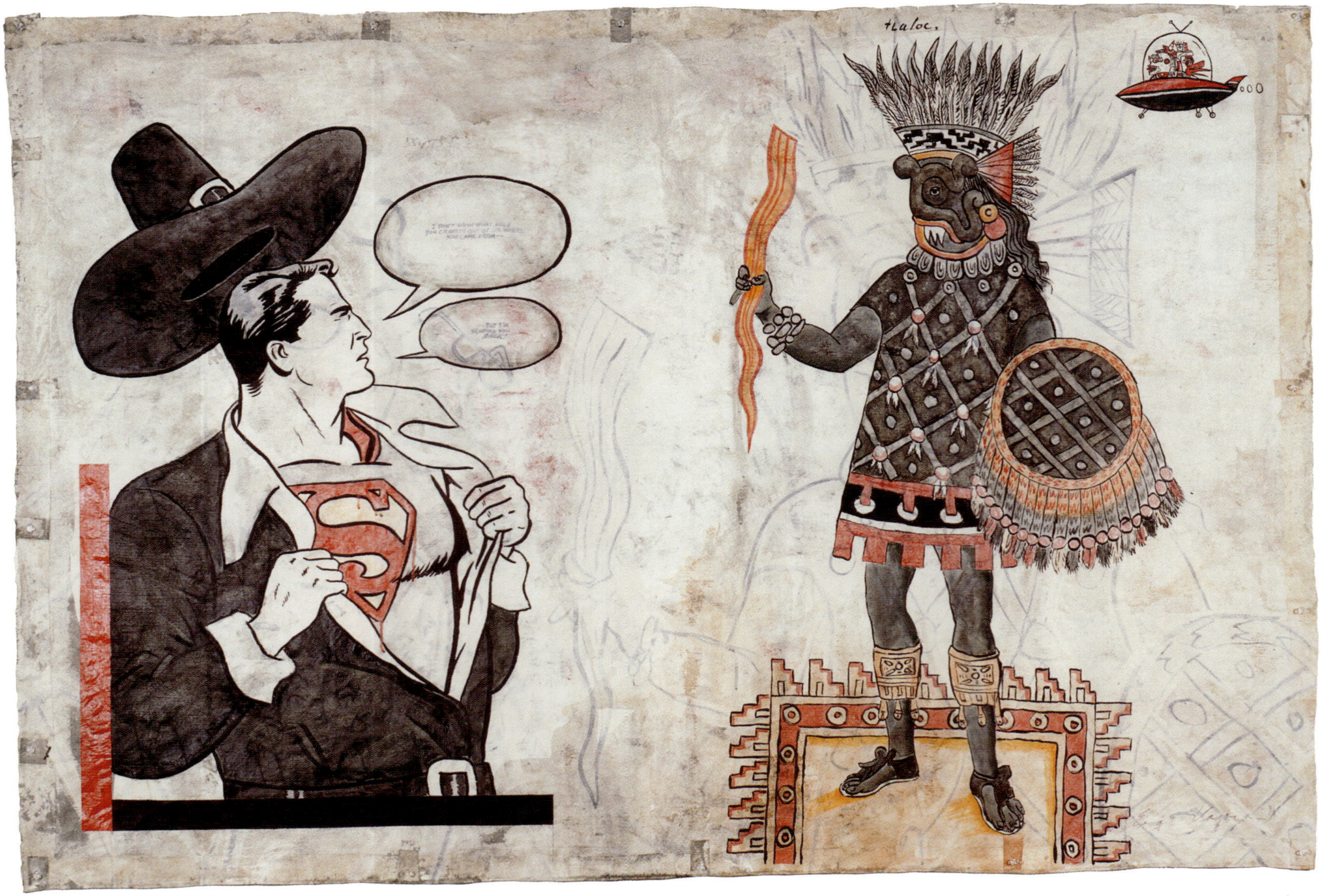

Crossing I, 1994

Acrylic and water based oil on Amate paper. 48 x 60 in.

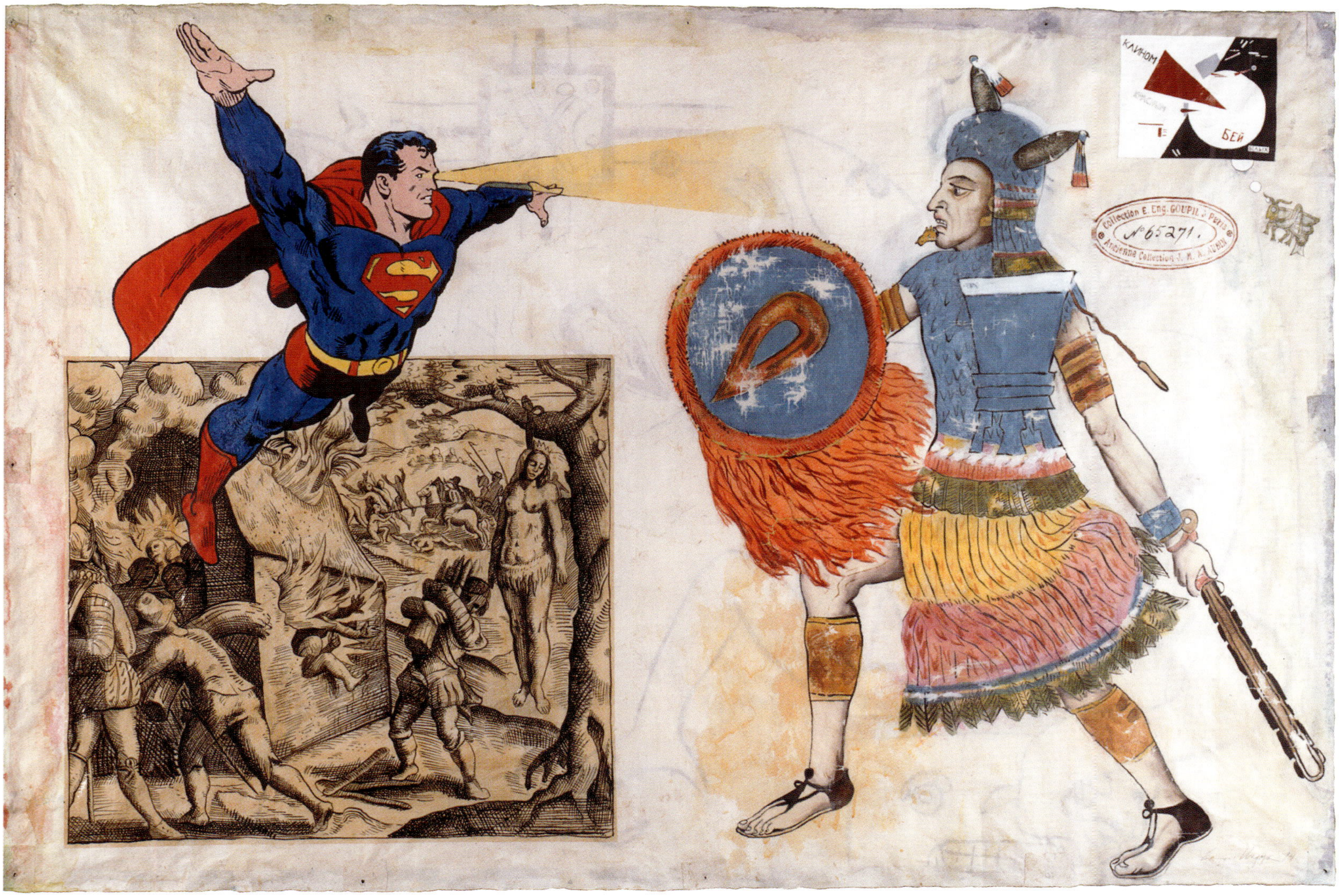

The Uprising of the Spirit, 1994

Acrylic and water based oil on Amate paper. 48 x 60 in.

There is a joke about Pancho Villa's skull: A little kid tries to sell a tourist a small human skull. He says to the tourist, "Hey mister, I am selling you Pancho Villa's skull. The tourist responds, "But you sold me Pancho Villa's skull last year and it was bigger. "Oh yes," the kid says, "but this one is from when he was a baby."

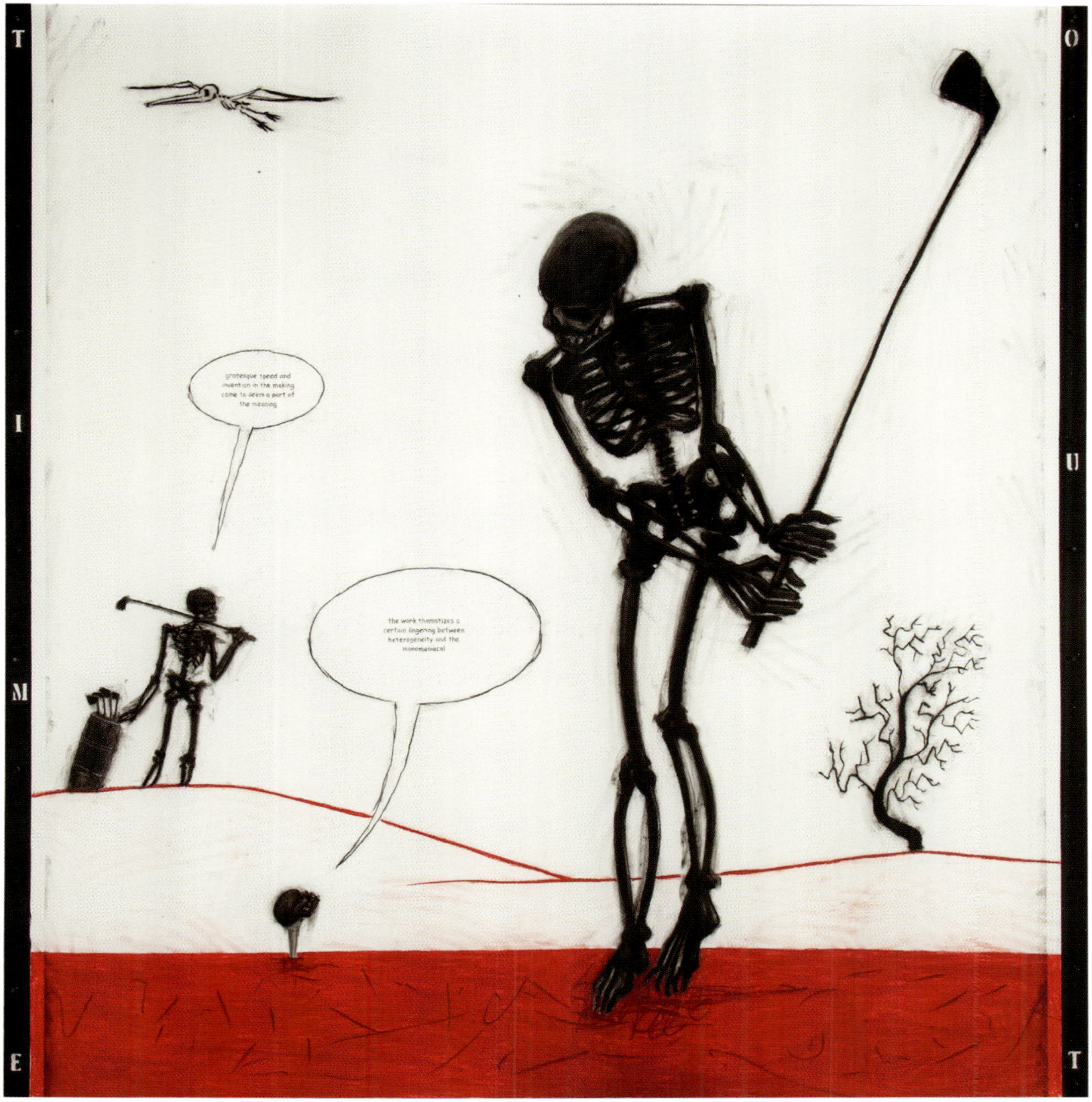

Time Out, 2009

Charcoal and pastel on paper. 80 x 80 in.

REVERSE Modernism

My work with reverse anthropology evolved into reverse modernism, which focuses on modern art. Picasso appropriated African masks and created Cubism, while Frank Lloyd Wright drew on Mayan architecture to develop some of his houses in Los Angeles. Aztec models influenced Henry Moore's sculptures. Some of the Surrealists thought that the "primitive" cultures were the childhood of humanity and that they were, like children, free to create. In my work I wonder what would happen if the "primitive" artists had discovered European art with the same admiration, perhaps without understanding, as that of Picasso and the others. I am not trashing Picasso, Henry Moore or Frank Lloyd Wright. I actually admire their art, but it does not stop me from trying to do the opposite in developing my own idea of reverse modernism.

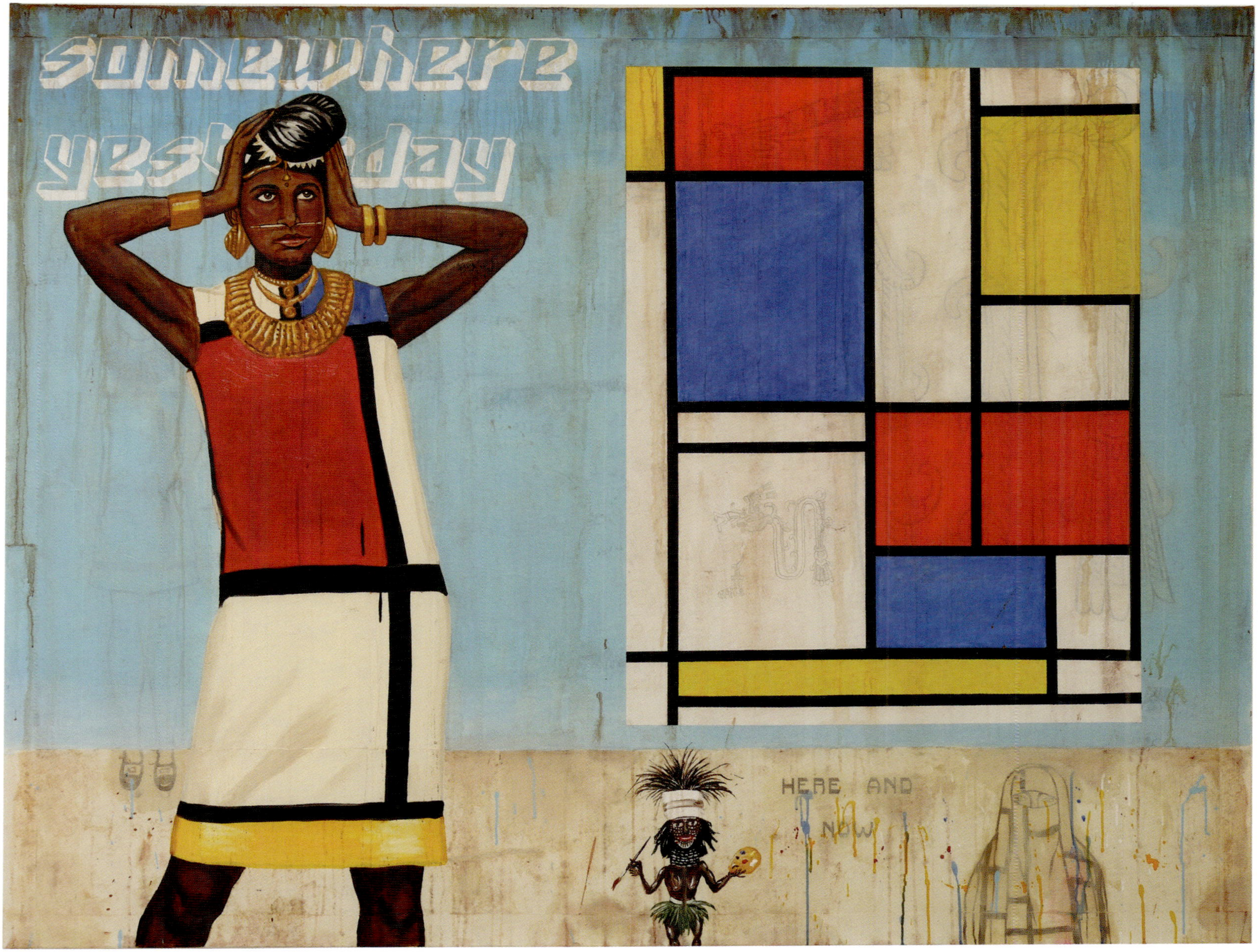

Somewhere Yesterday, 2016

Acrylic and water based oil on Amate paper mounted on canvas. 60 x 80 in.

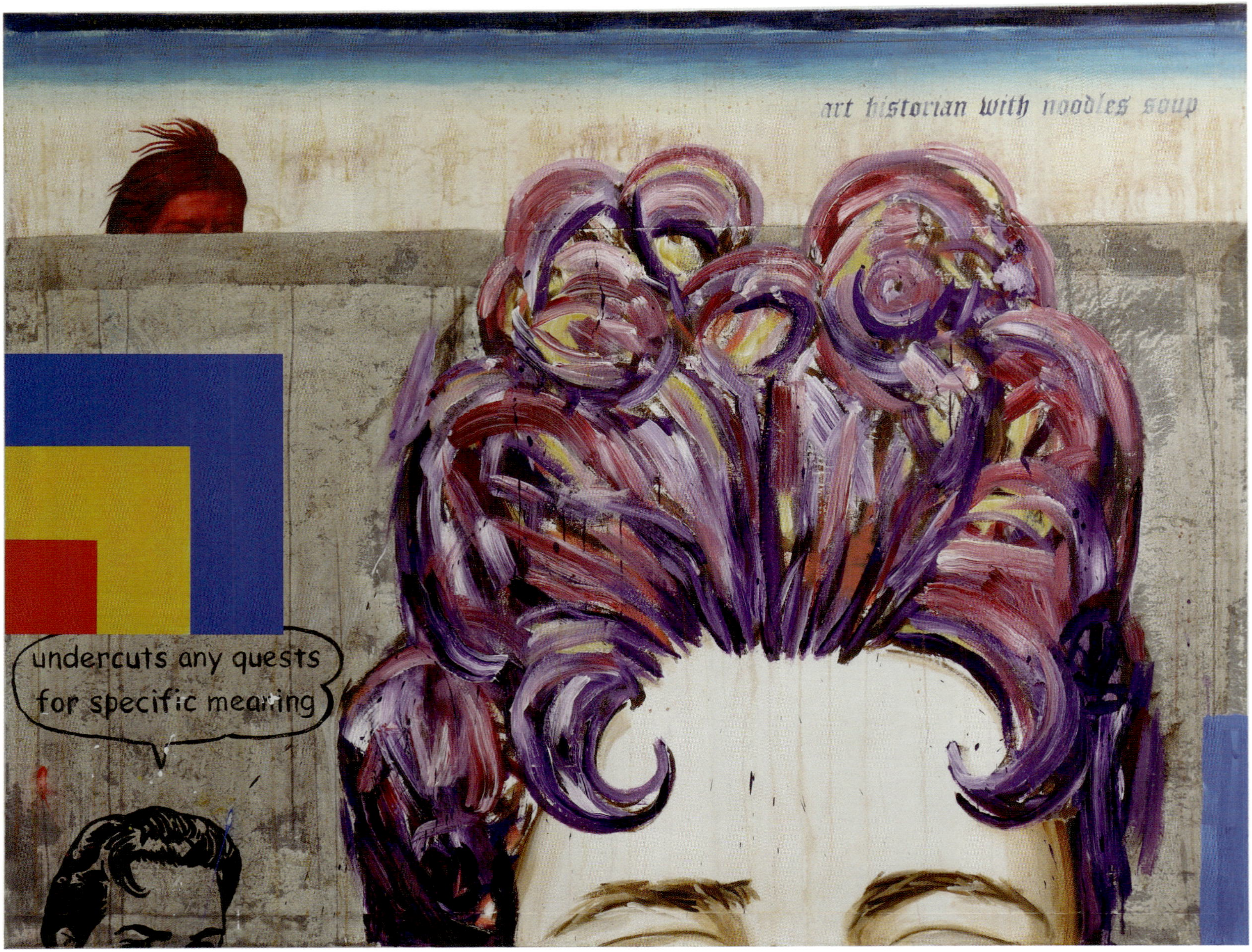

Art Historian with Noodles Soup, 2013–2016

Acrylic and water based oil on Amate paper mounted on canvas. 60 x 80 in.

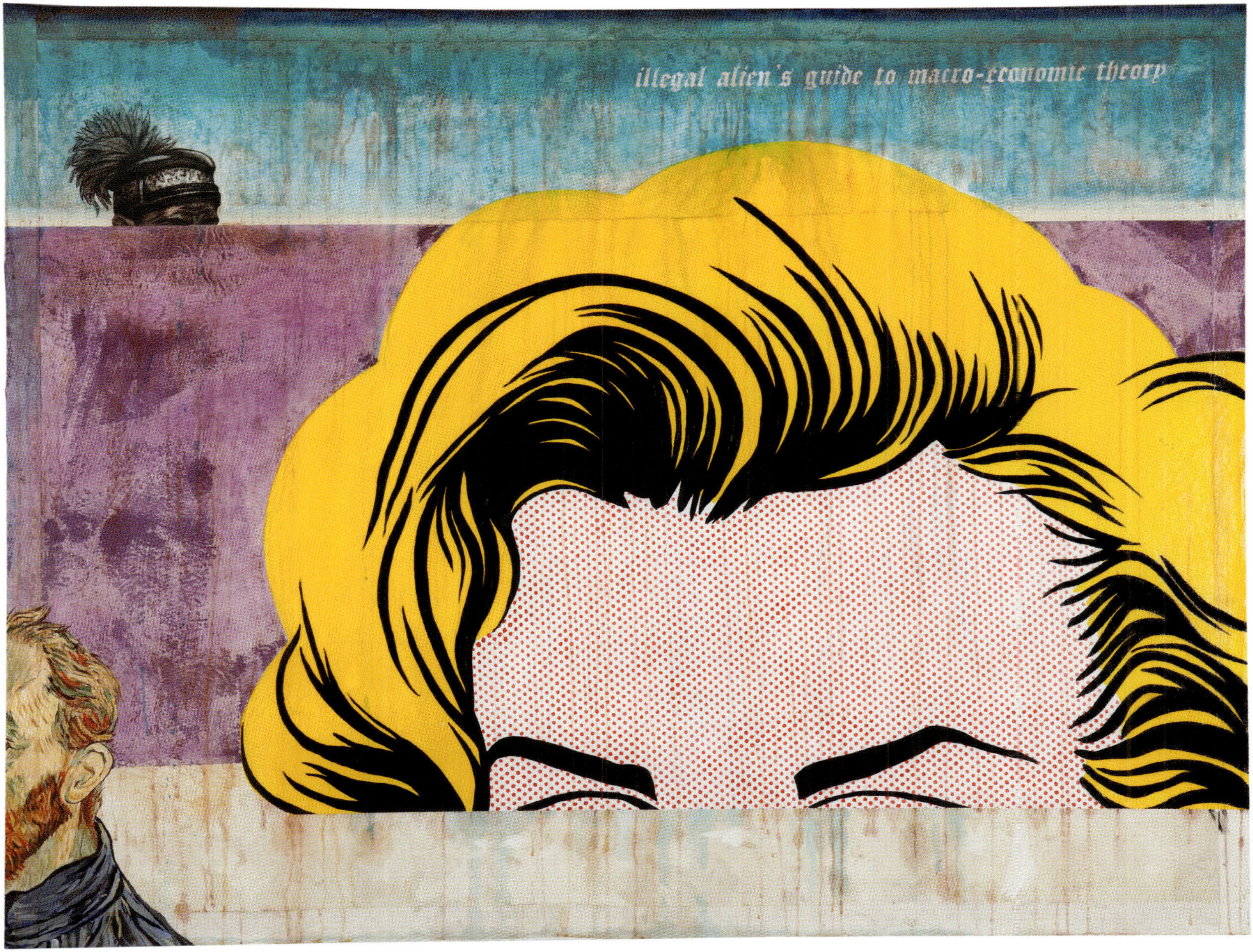

Illegal Alien's Guide to Macroeconomic Theory, 2013
Acrylic and water based oil on Amate paper mounted on canvas. 60 x 80 in.

Very often I appropriate modernist art with an indigenous or "primitive" twist. It could be an artist from Africa or different indigenous cultures in the Americas or New Guinea or Asia. Wherever there was a colony and there was art. I am trying to reverse that appropriation of European art, and that is where my skills of appropriating look-alike forgeries come to life.

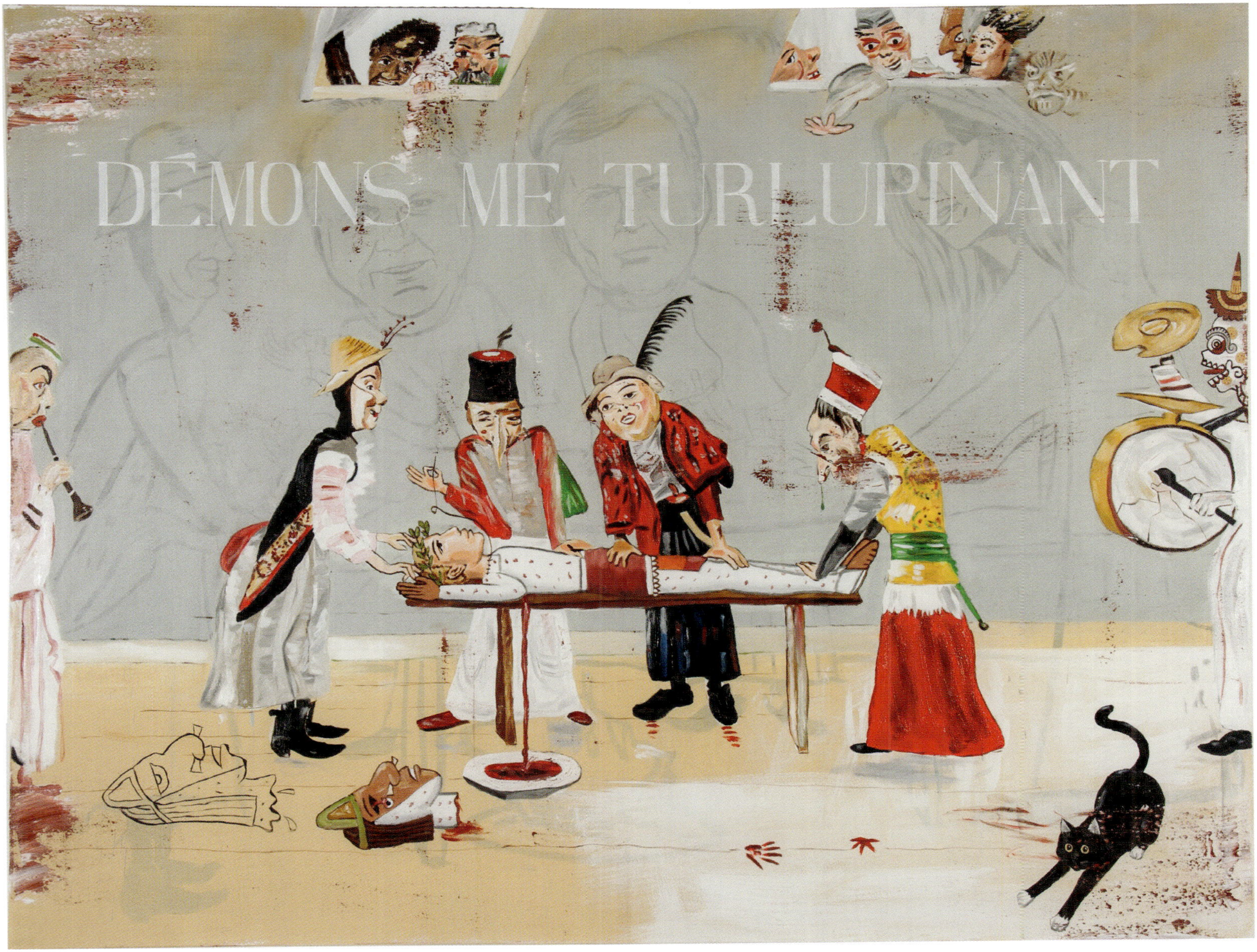

Thinking of Ensor and My Cat Diego, 2009
Acrylic and water based oil on canvas. 60 x 80 in.

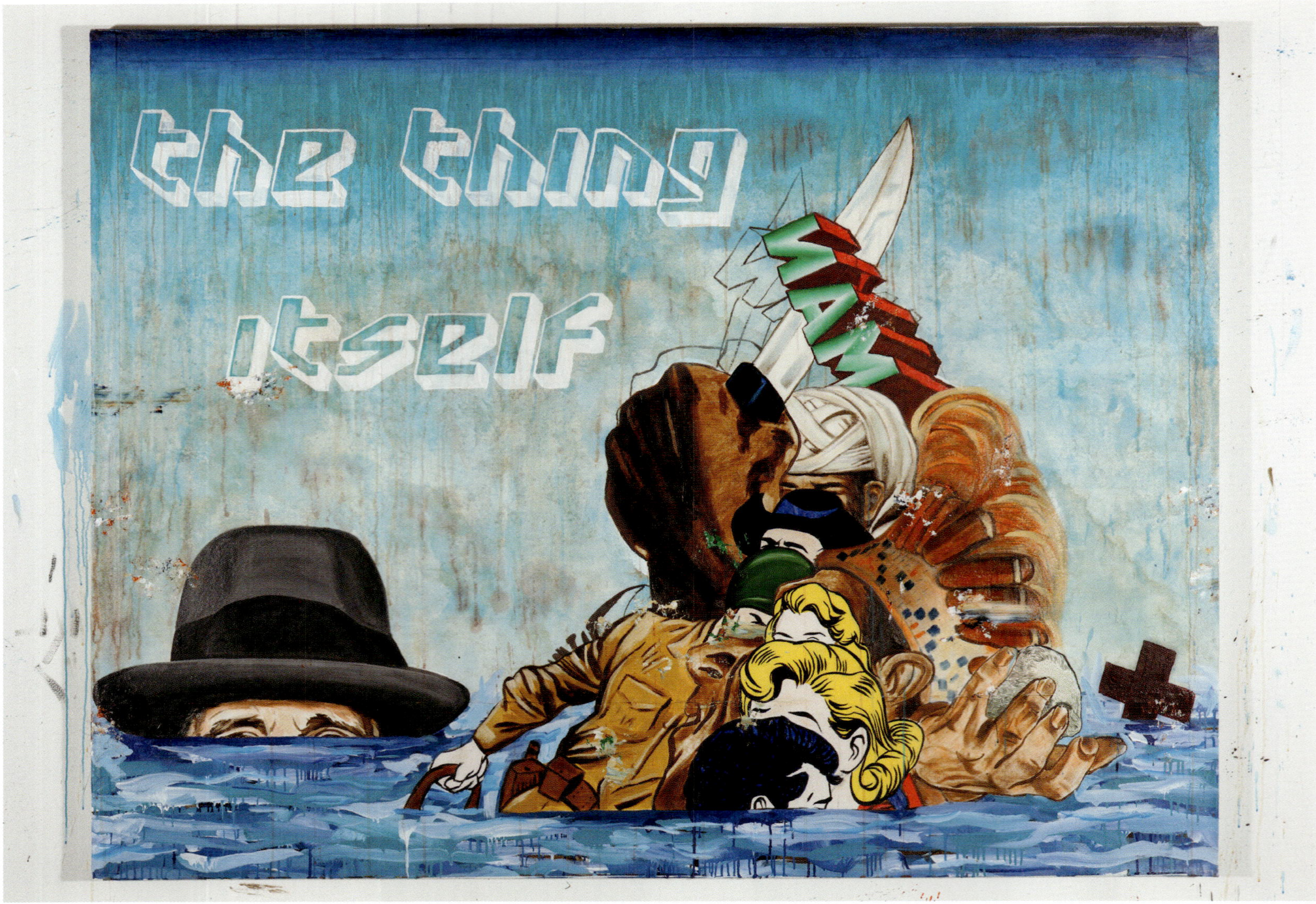

The Thing Itself, 2013

Acrylic and water based oil on Amate paper mounted on canvas. 60 x 80 in.

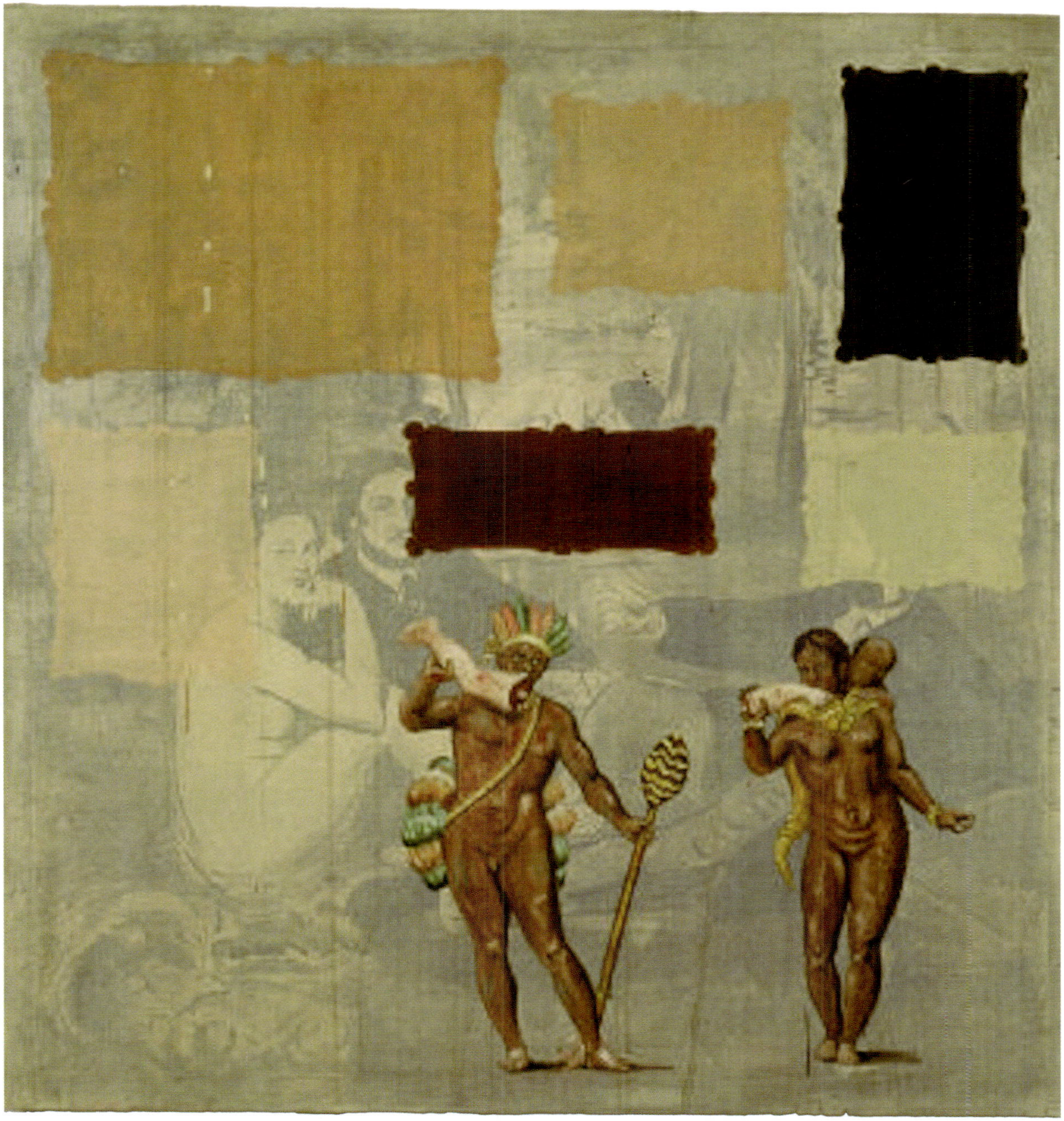

An Object at the Limits of Language, 2000
Acrylic and water based oil on Amate paper mounted on canvas. 60 x 80 in.

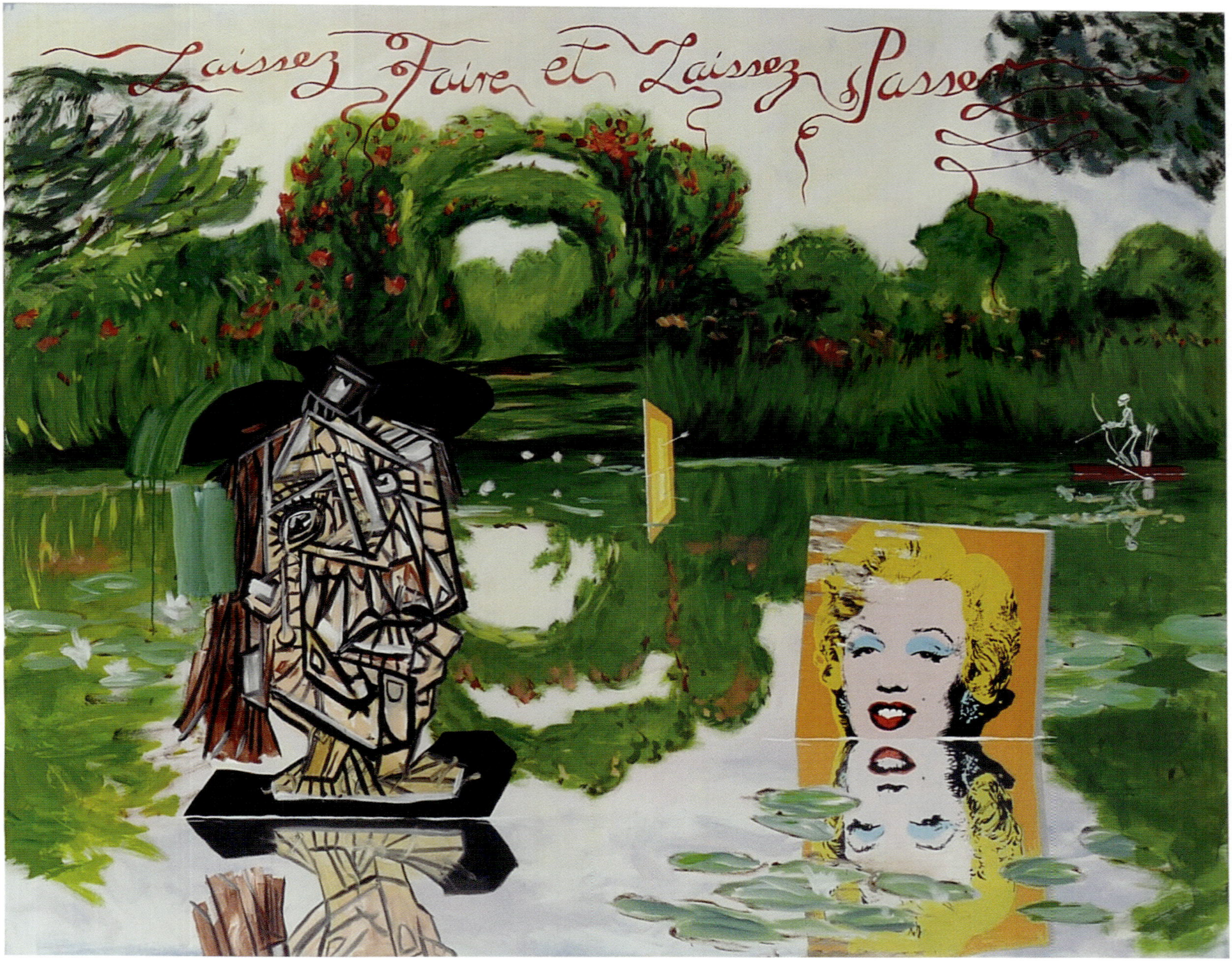

Auction House Blues, 2009–2016

Acrylic and water based oil on canvas. 60 x 80 in.

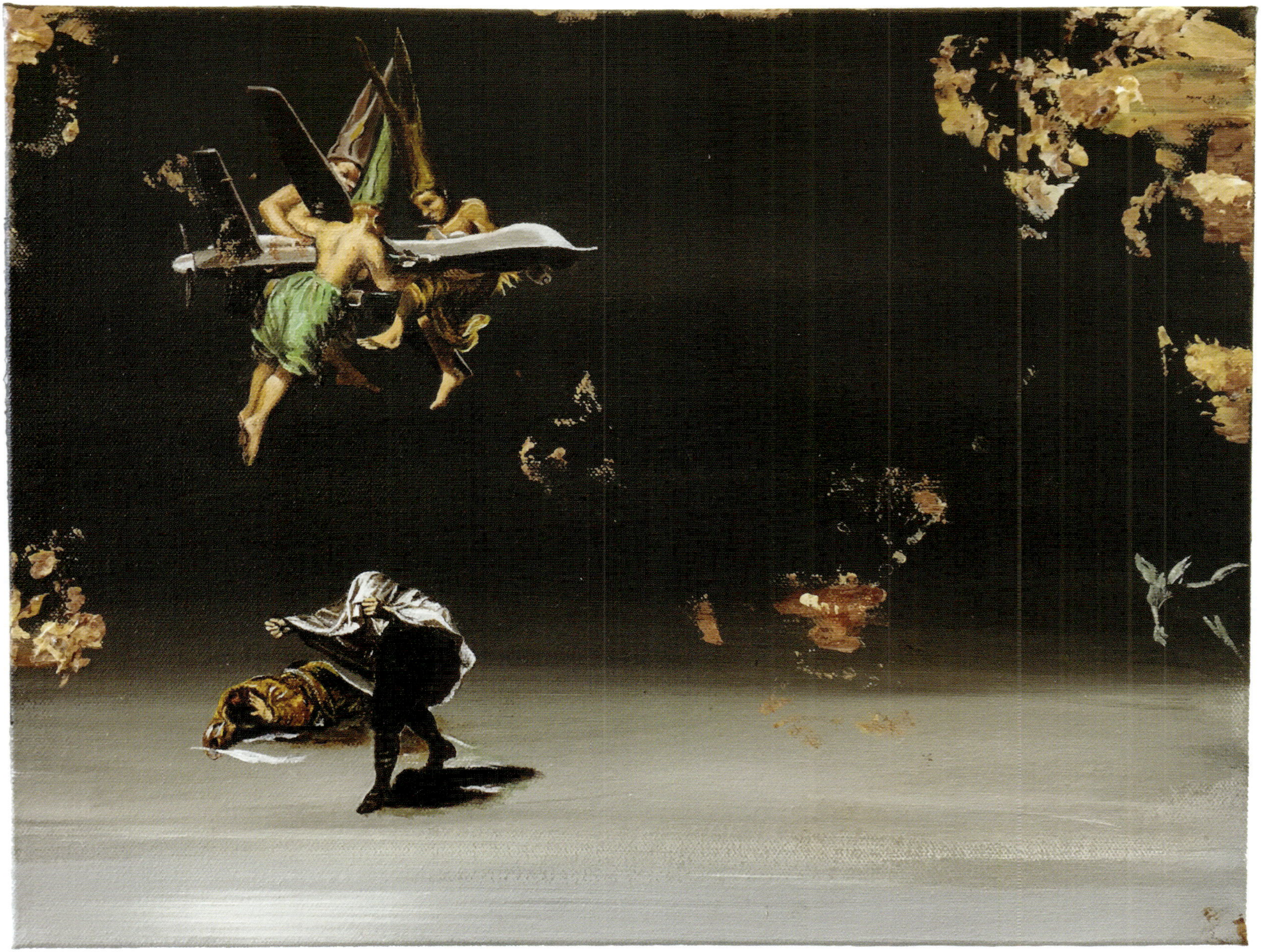

Goya's Witches Save the Day, 2018
Acrylic, water based oil on canvas with collaged glass eye. 16 x 20 in.

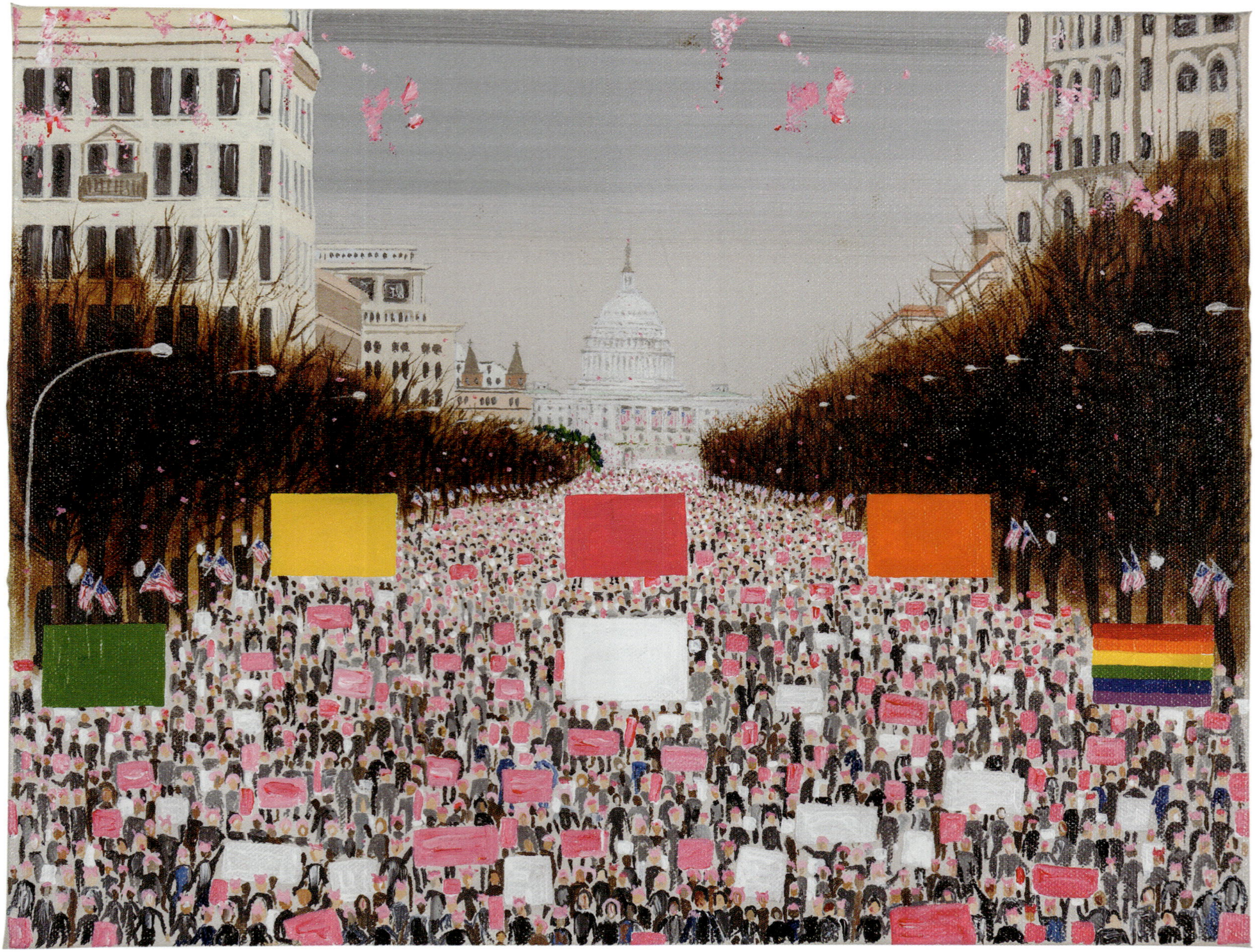

The Day After, 2018

Acrylic and water based oil on canvas. 16 x 20 in.

Acknowledgments

*To my wife, artist Kara Maria, for her love,
inspiration and support, and for teaching me
to appreciate all animals (besides my fellow humans)
and our fragile planet's ecosystems.*

Photography credits:
Eugenio Castro
Wolfgang Dietze
Rubén Guzmán

Thanks to:
Magnolia Editions, Oakland, CA
Shark's Ink, Lyons, CO
Anglim Gilbert Gallery, San Francisco, CA
Lisa Sette Gallery, Phoenix, AZ
George Adams Gallery, New York, NY
Stanford University's Department of Art and Art History, Stanford, CA

Enrique Chagoya

American, born in Mexico City, Mexico
Lives in San Francisco, California

Enrique Chagoya was born and raised in Mexico City. His father, a Banco de México employee by day and artist by night, encouraged his interest in art by teaching Chagoya color theory and how to sketch at a very early age. Chagoya studied political economy at Universidad Nacional Autónoma de México, where he contributed political cartoons to union newsletters. After university he relocated to Veracruz and directed a team focused on rural-development projects. Chagoya moved to Berkeley, California, at age 26, and worked as a freelance illustrator and graphic designer. He earned a BFA from the San Francisco Art Institute, in 1984, his MA and MFA at the University of California, Berkeley, in 1987, and an honorary doctorate from the San Francisco Art Institute in 2017.

Chagoya has been exhibiting his work nationally and internationally for over two decades. A major retrospective, "Borderlandia," was organized by the Des Moines Art Center in 2007. It traveled to the UC Berkeley Art Museum and to the Palm Springs Art Museum in 2008. In 2013 his first major traveling survey in Europe, "Palimpsesto Canibal/Cannibal Palimpsest," opened at the Artium Museum in Vitoria-Gasteiz in the Basque Country and, in 2015, at Centro Atlántico de Arte Moderno (CAAM) in the Canary Islands. Also that year a traveling print component from the retrospective opened at Instituto de Artes Gráficas de Oaxaca (IAGO); it traveled to the Museo Nacional de la Estampa (MUNAE) in Mexico City in the winter of 2016. The same year Chagoya had a solo exhibition at Anglim Gilbert Gallery in San Francisco. In 2017 he was included in an exhibition of American Pop art that opened in the winter at the British Museum in London. In 2018 he had exhibitions at the Cathy and Jesse Marion Art Gallery at SUNY Fredonia, the Nevada Museum of Art in Reno, and the George Adams Gallery in NYC.

Chagoya is currently Full Professor at Stanford University's Department of Art and Art History. His work is in many public collections, including the Museum of Modern Art, New York, Metropolitan Museum of Art, Whitney Museum of American Art, San Francisco Museum of Modern Art, Fine Arts Museums of San Francisco, Museo Nacional de la Estampa, Instituto de Artes Gráficas de Oaxaca and Fundación Televisa in Mexico, and Artium Museum in Vitoria-Gasteiz in Spain. He is the recipient of two NEA artist fellowships, a fellowship from the National Academy of Arts and Letters in New York, and residencies at Giverny and Cité Internationale des Arts in France.

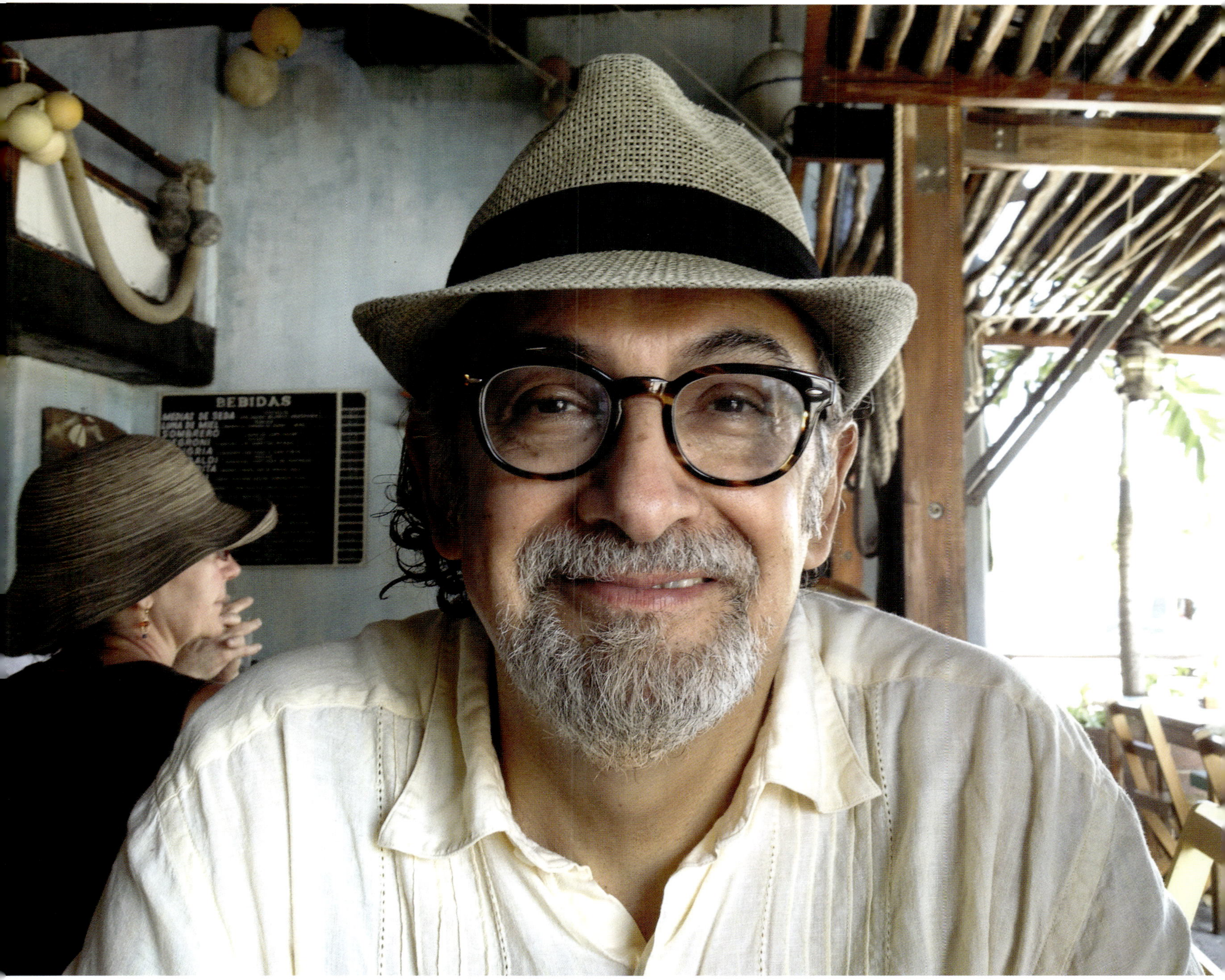

Enrique Chagoya. Photo by Kara Maria 2014

Please **turn** to the last book page to start the **Codices.**

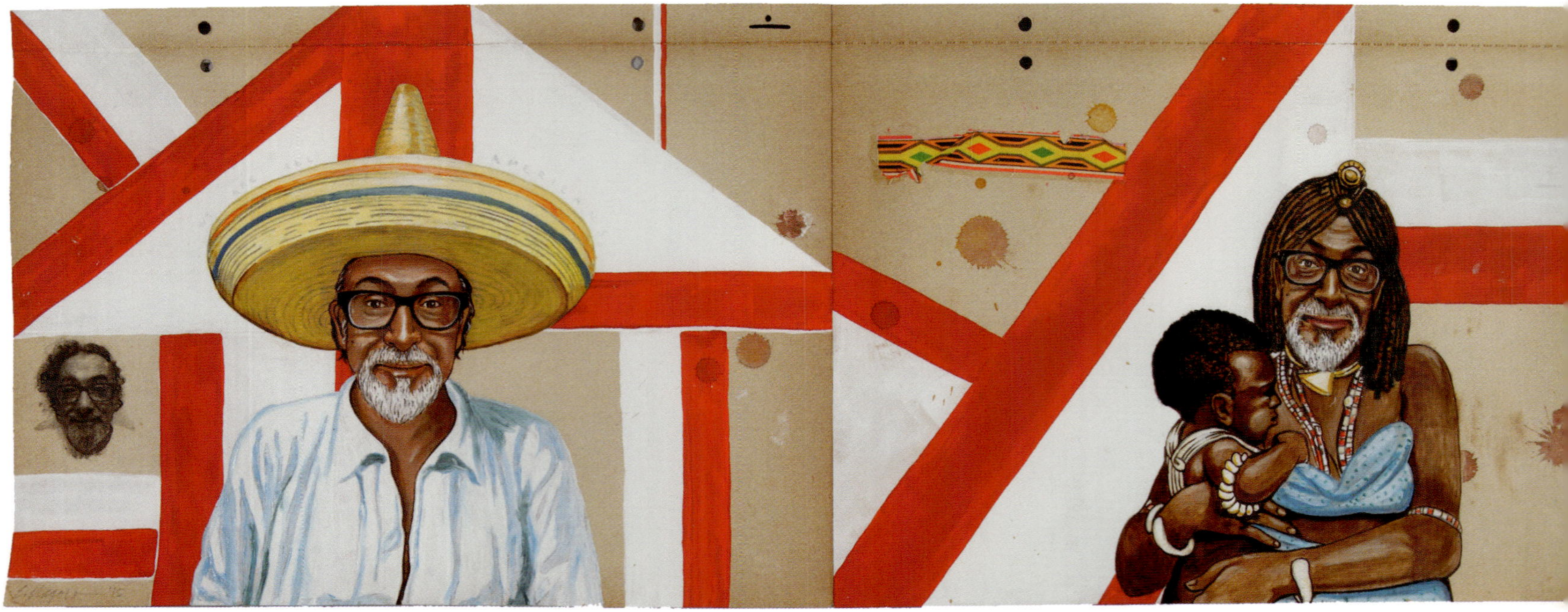

ALIeNS

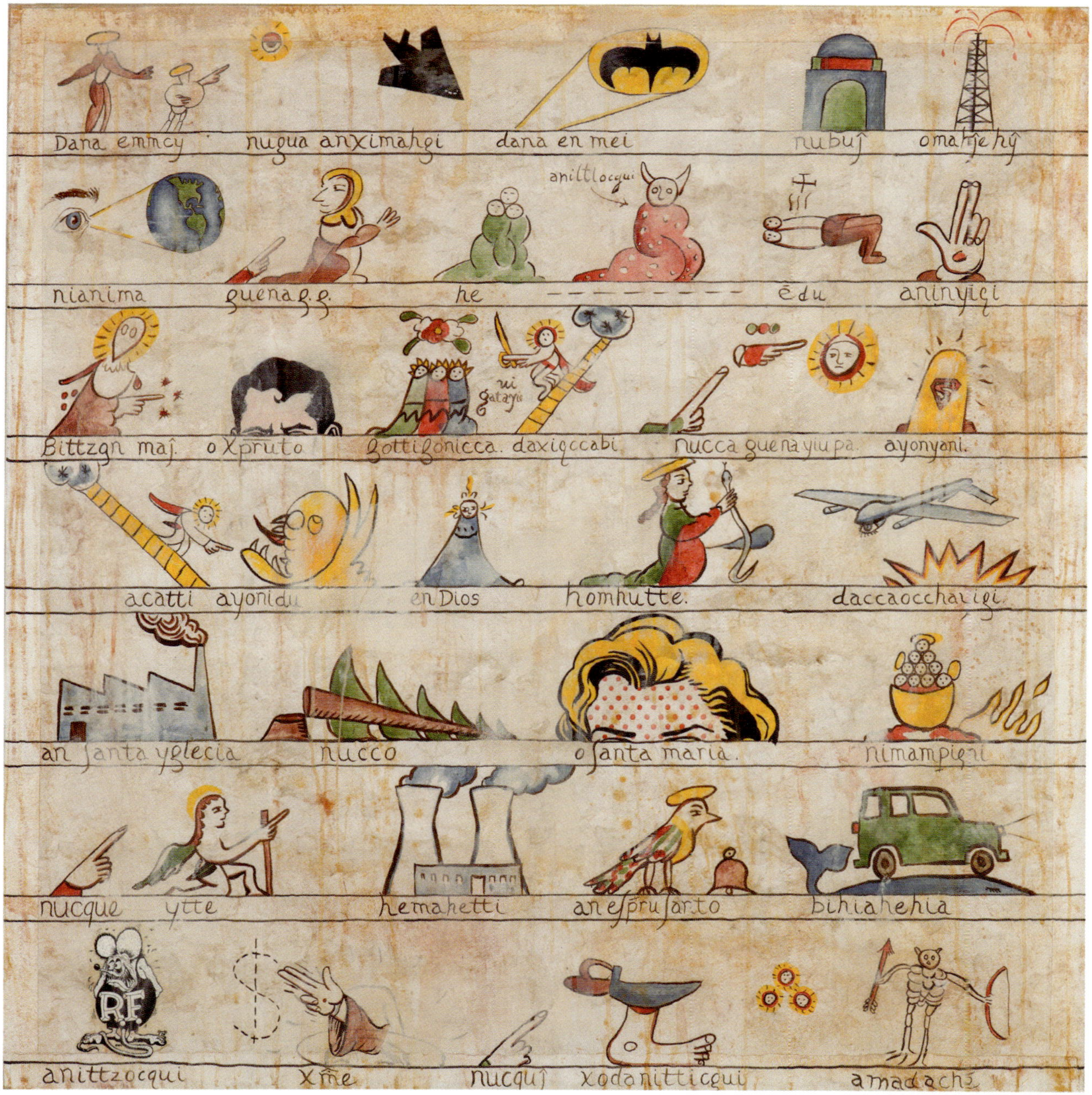

Codex Finalis Chronos, 2013

Acrylic, water based oil and decal on handmade Amate paper mounted on canvas. 48 x 48 in.

ALIeNS

Art and Text by Enrique Chagoya

Edited by Bart Schneider

Kelly's Cove Press

CODICES

I began to work on codices when I learned about the destruction of the pre-Columbian books that took place during the conquest of Mexico City (the ancient city Tenochtitlan), the Mayan territory and the Mixtex Zapotec territory in the southern part of Oaxaca. These cultures—the Aztecs, the Nahua Indians, the Mayans in the Yucatán and Central America, and the Mixtec Zapotec—had thousands of books and had been producing books for centuries. They had a giant library in Mexico City in the Aztec kingdom of Texcoco, which was one of three kingdoms in Mexico City: Tlatelolco, Texcoco and Tenochtitlan.

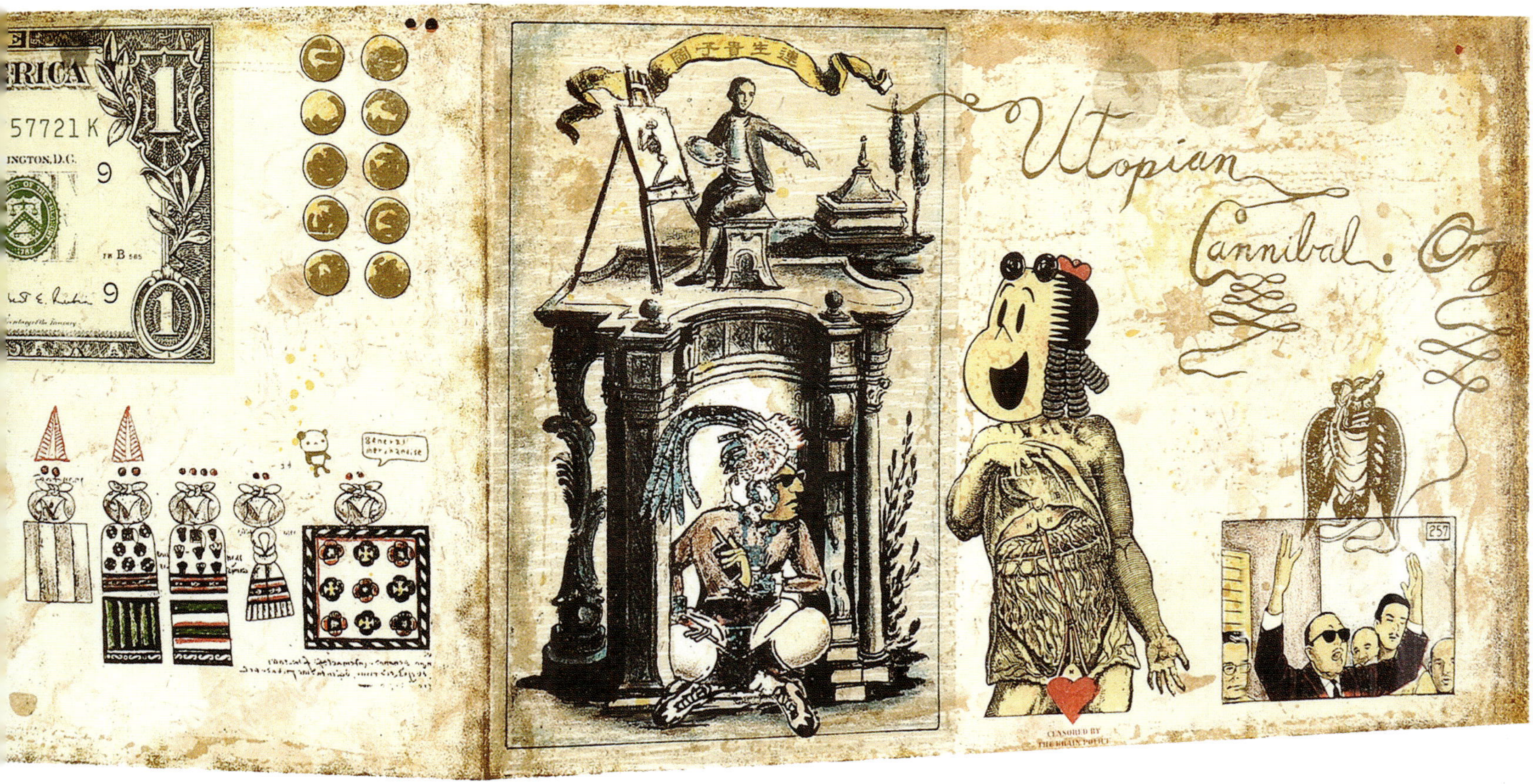

UtopianCannibal.org, 2000

Color lithograph with chine collé and collaged eyes. 7 1/2 x 92 in.

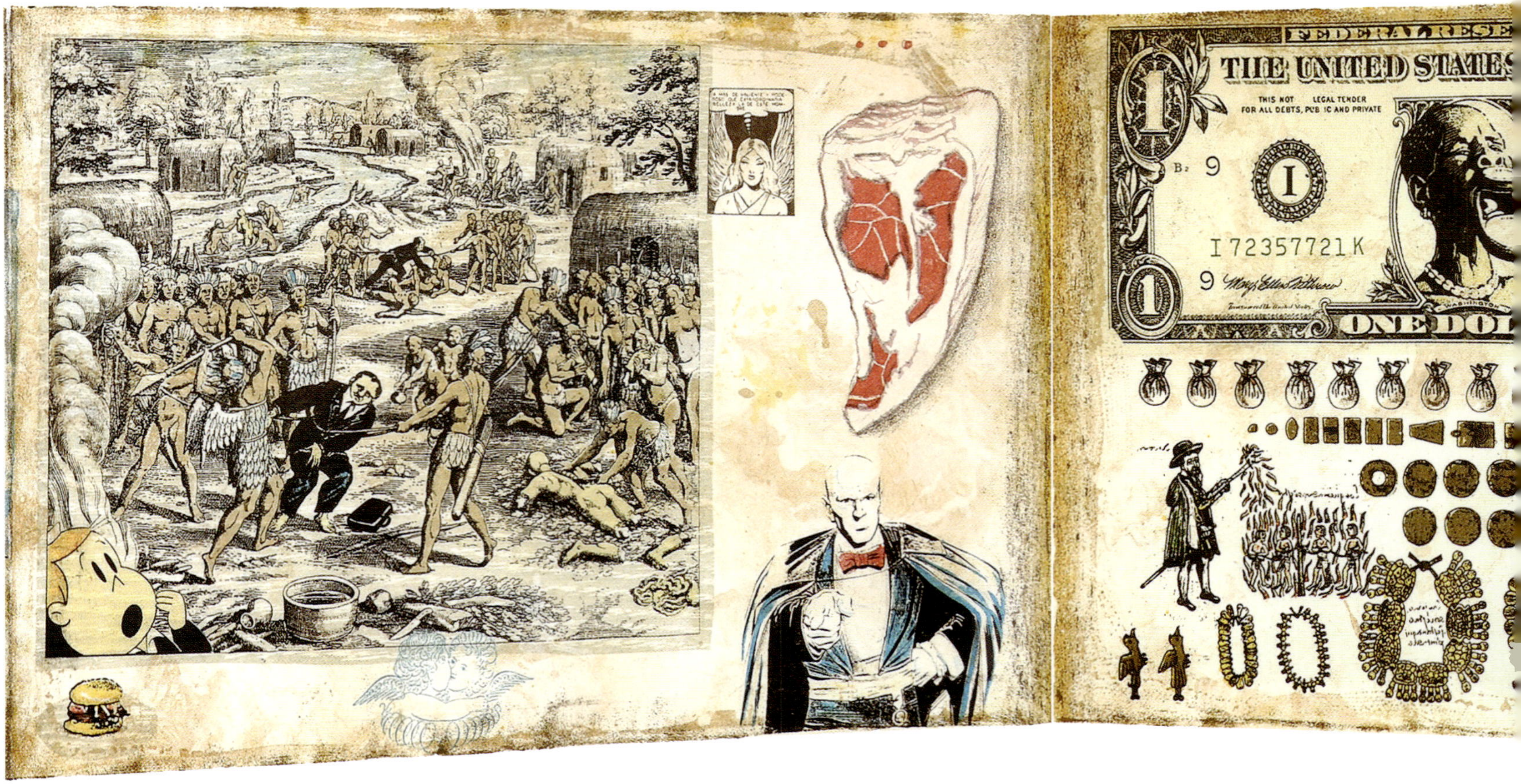
FEDERAL RESE
THE UNITED STATES
THIS NOT LEGAL TENDER
FOR ALL DEBTS, PUB IC AND PRIVATE
B2 9
I
I72357721K
9
WASHINGTON
ONE DOL

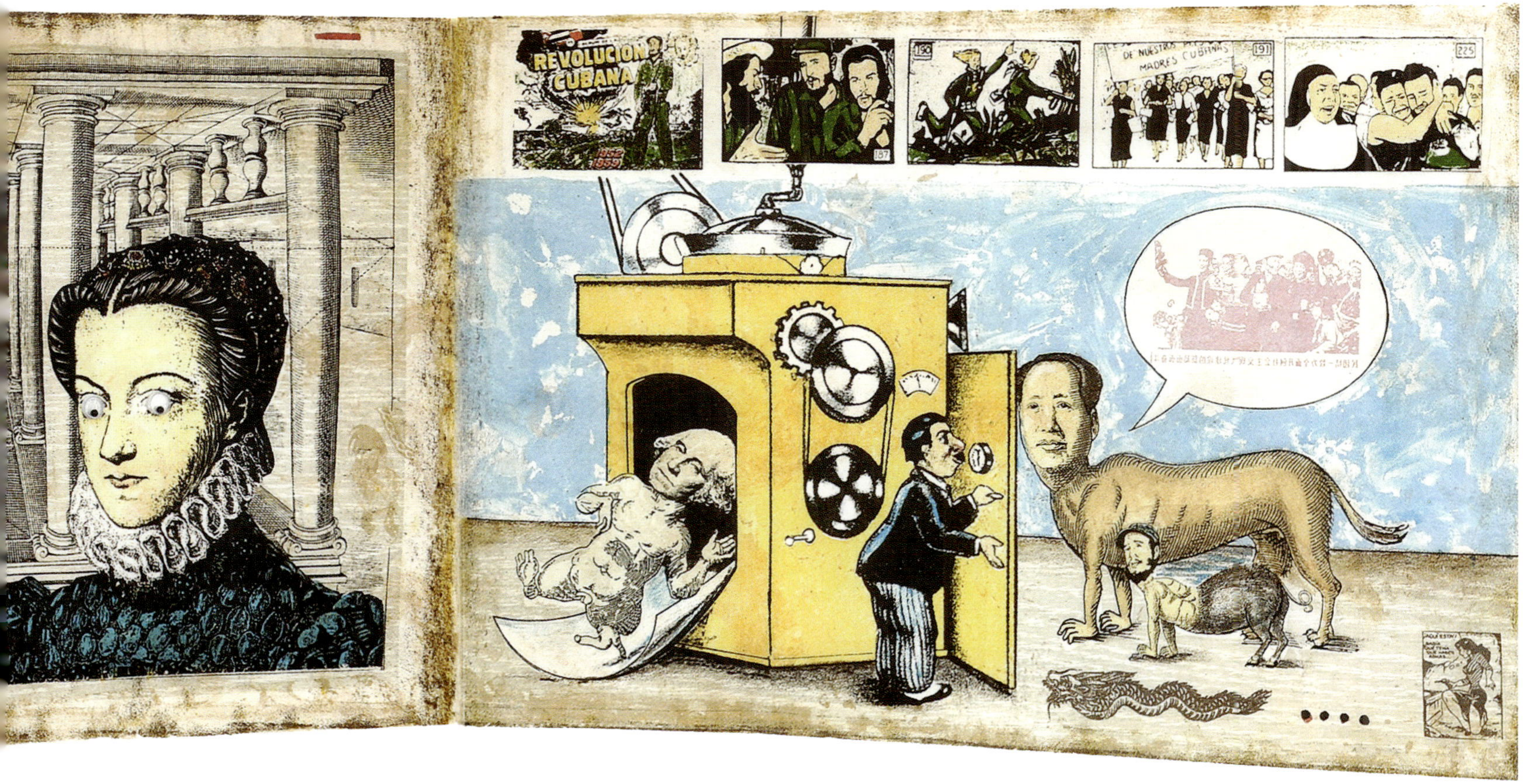

UtopianCannibal.org

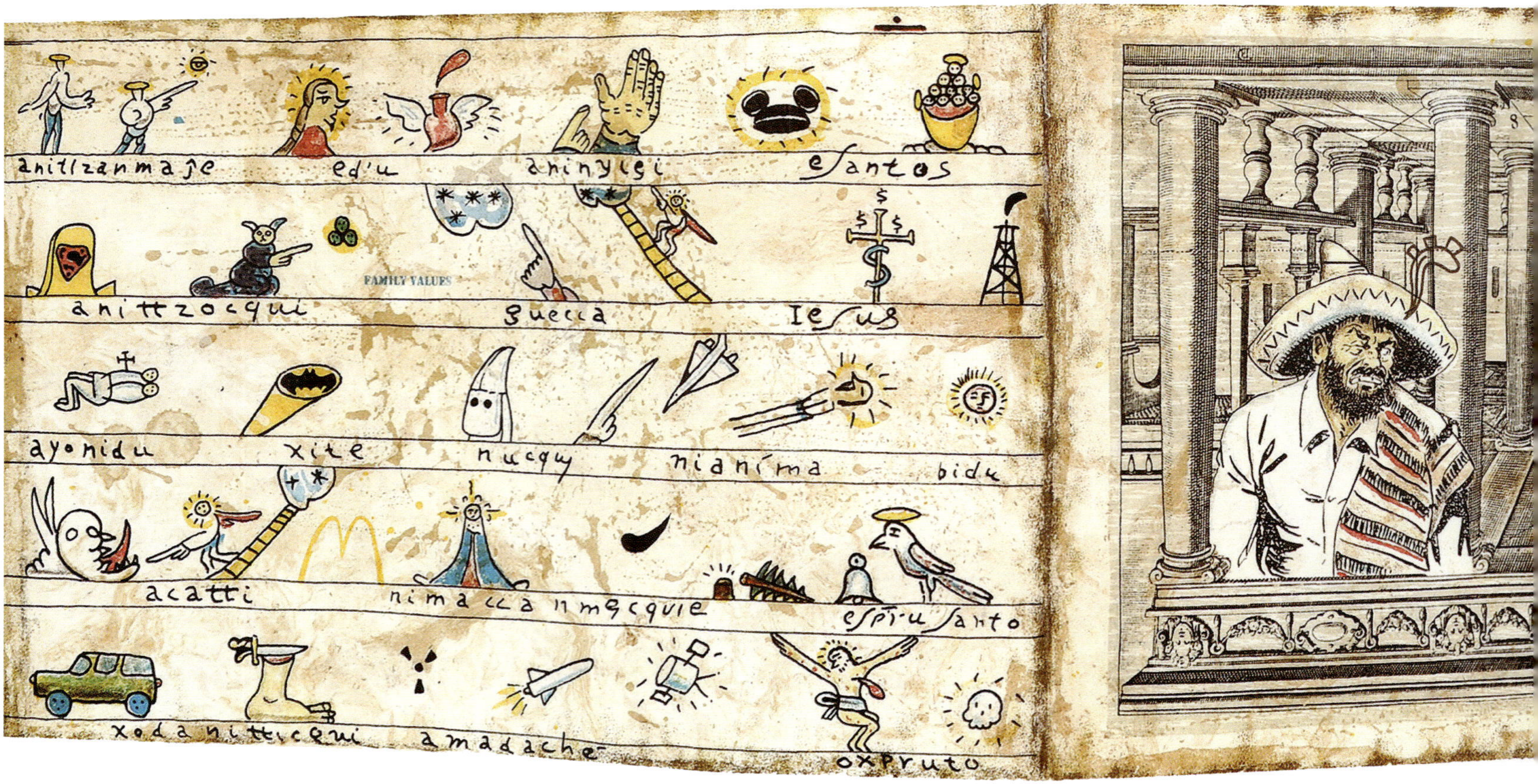
anitizanmaje
ed'u
aninyigi
esantos
FAMILY VALUES
anittzocqui
guecca
Iesus
ayonidu
xite
nucqu
nianima
bidu
acatti
nimaccanmecquie
espiru santo
amadache
oxpruto

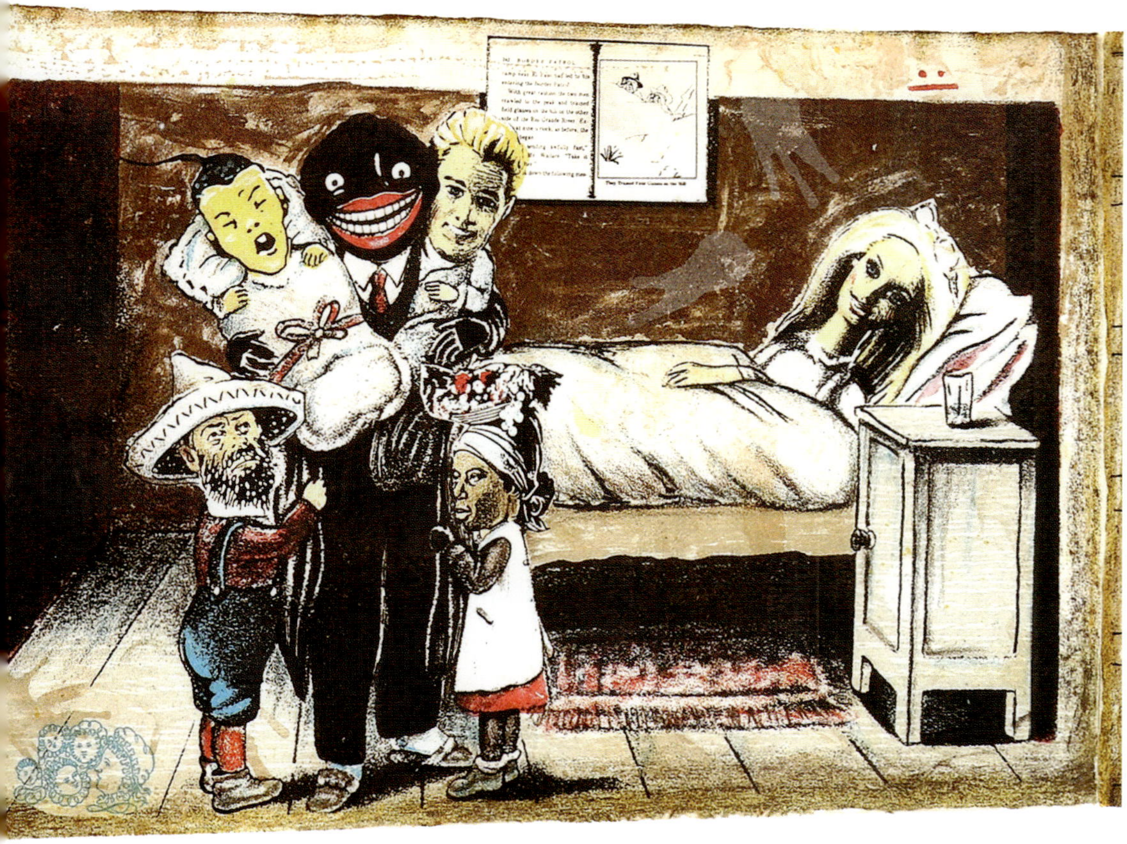

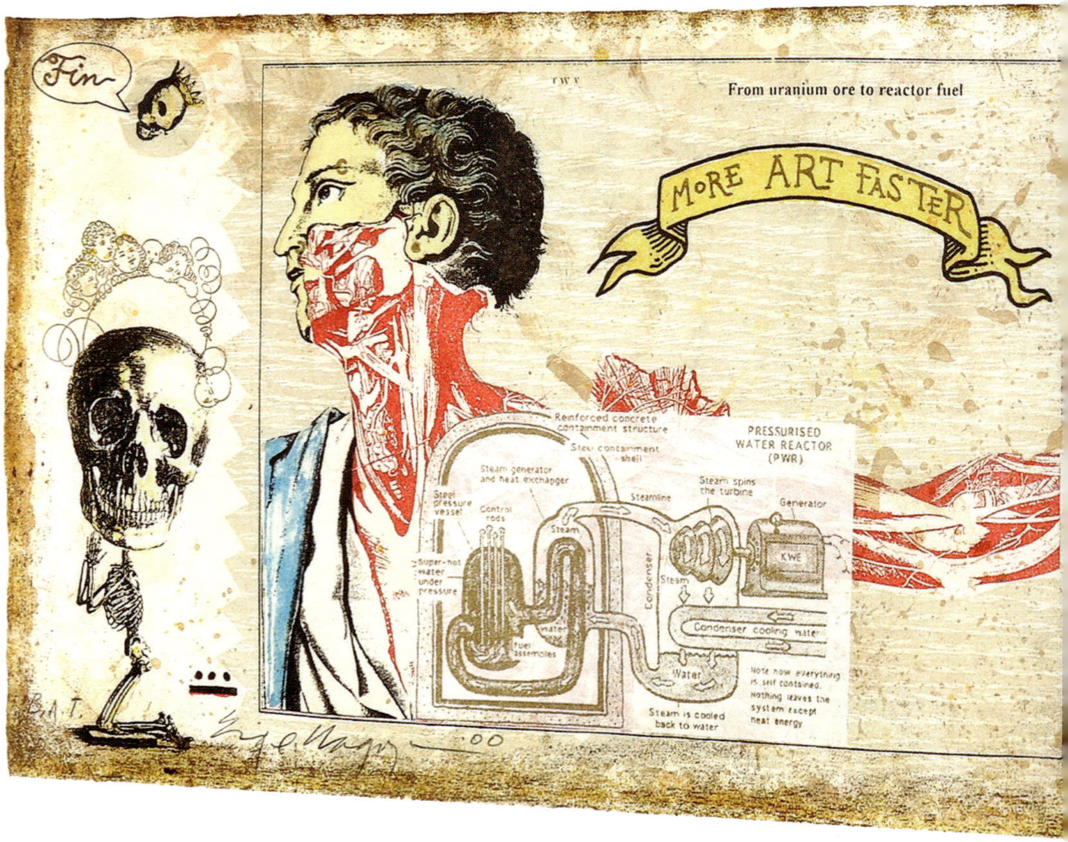
Fin
From uranium ore to reactor fuel
MORE ART FASTER
Reinforced concrete containment structure
Steel containment shell
PRESSURISED WATER REACTOR (PWR)
Steam generator and heat exchanger
Steel pressure vessel
Control rods
Steamline
Steam spins the turbine
Generator
Steam
Super-hot water under pressure
Condenser
KWE
Water
Fuel assemblies
Condenser cooling water
Water
Note how everything is self contained. Nothing leaves the system except heat energy
Steam is cooled back to water
B.A.T.

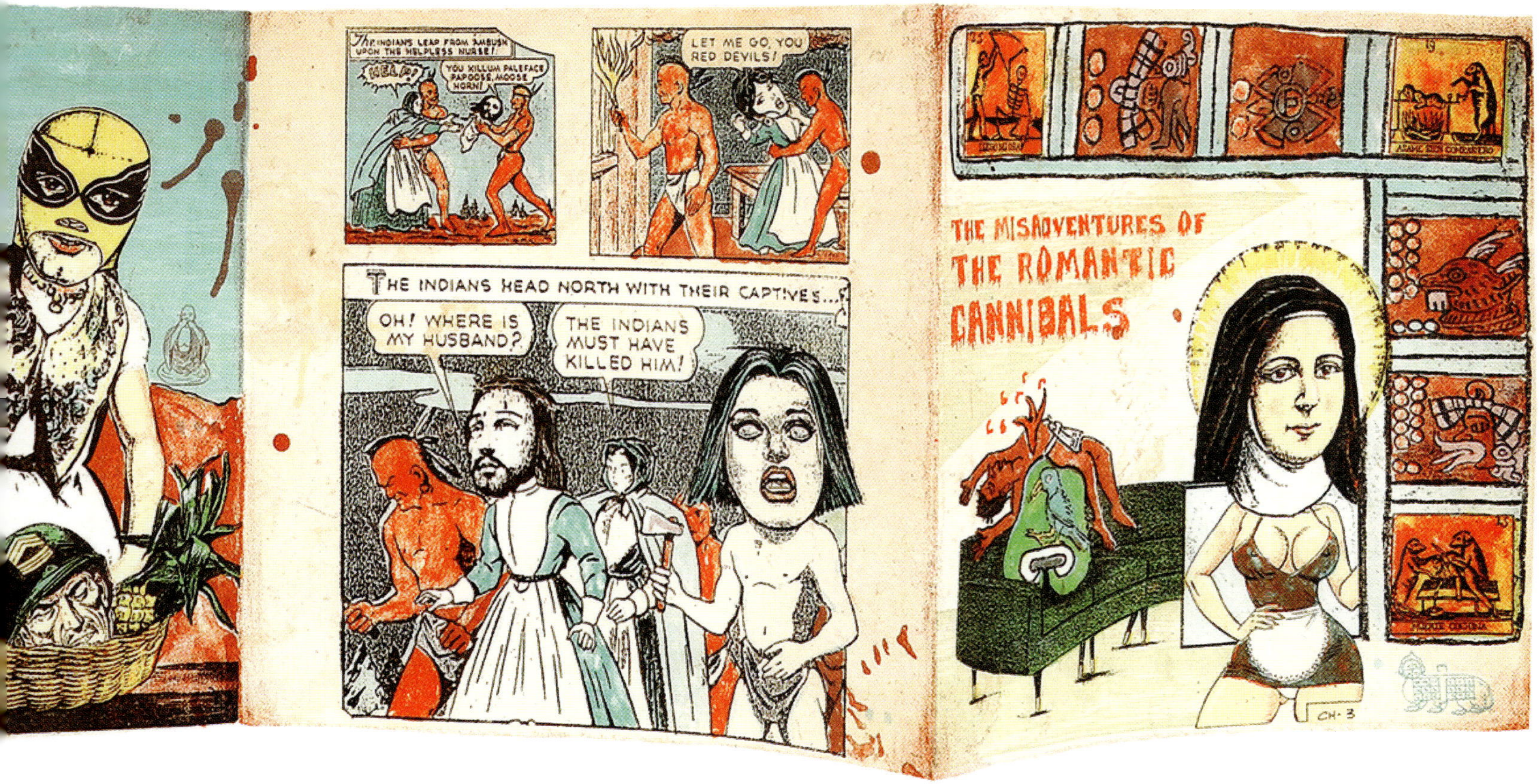

The Misadventures of the Romantic Cannibals, 2002
Color lithograph and woodcut. 7 1/2 x 90 in.

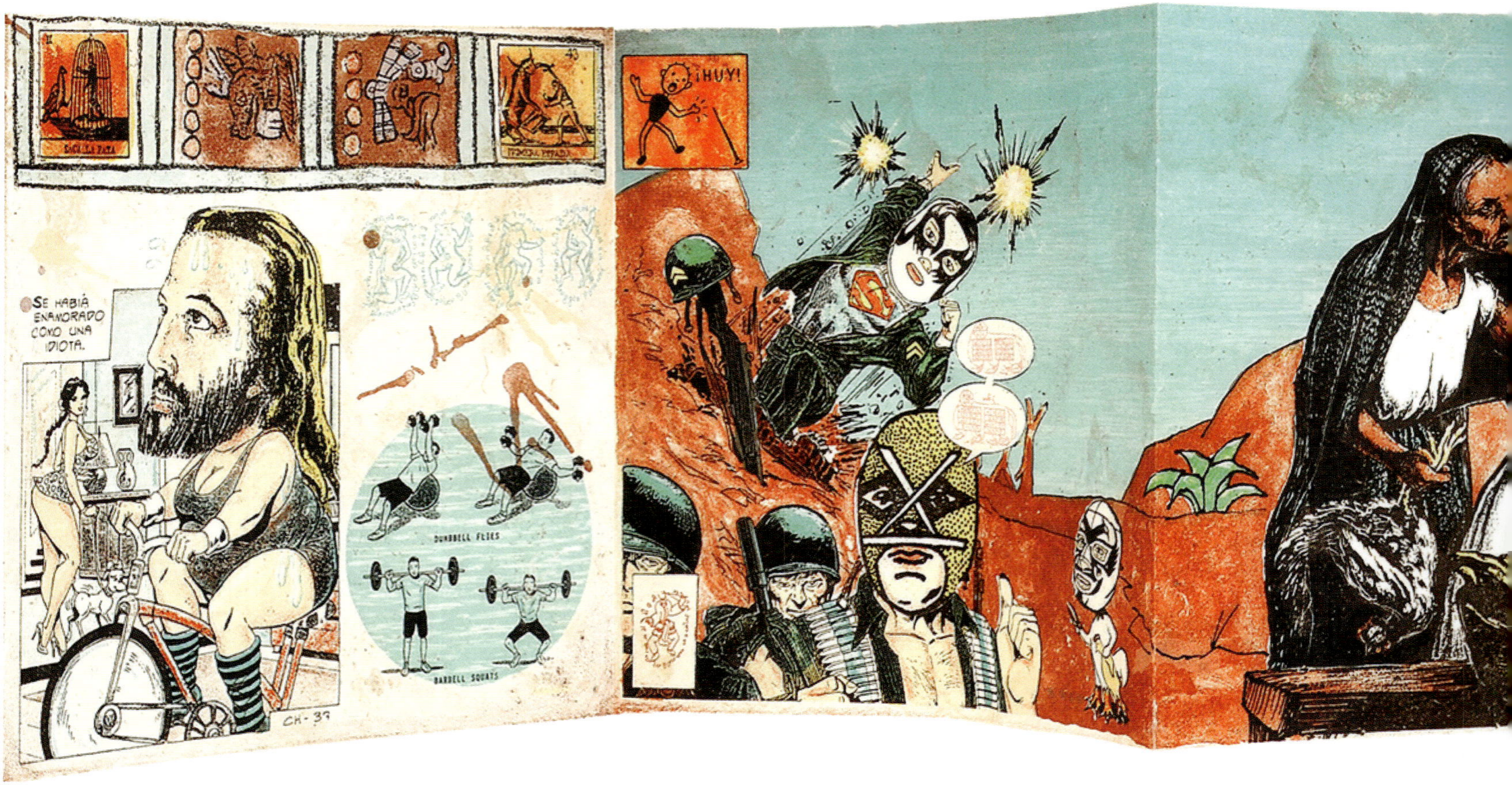
SE HABIÁ ENAMORADO COMO UNA IDIOTA.
DUMBBELL FLIES
BARBELL SQUATS
CH-37
¡HUY!

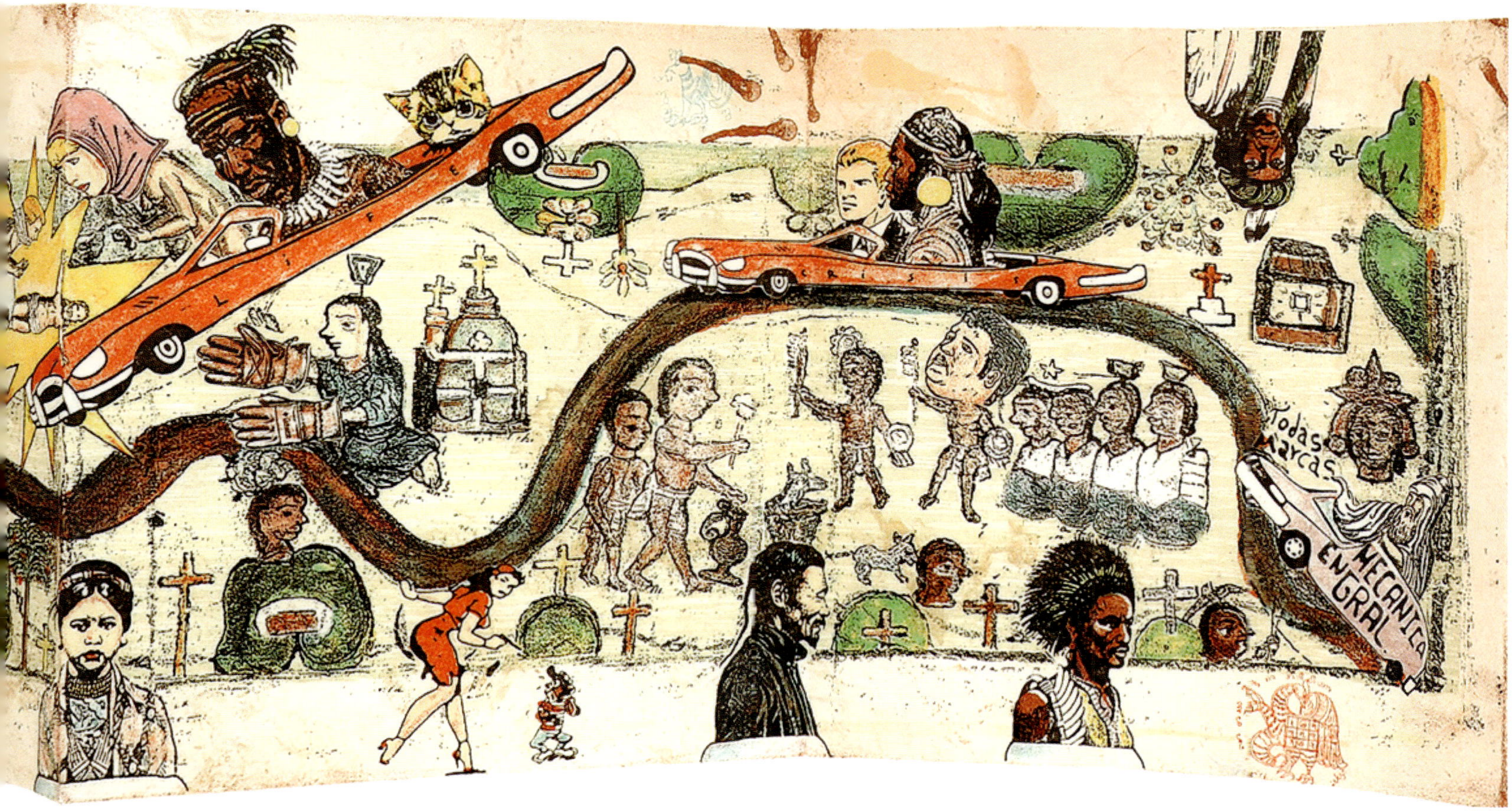

The Misadventures of the Romantic Cannibals

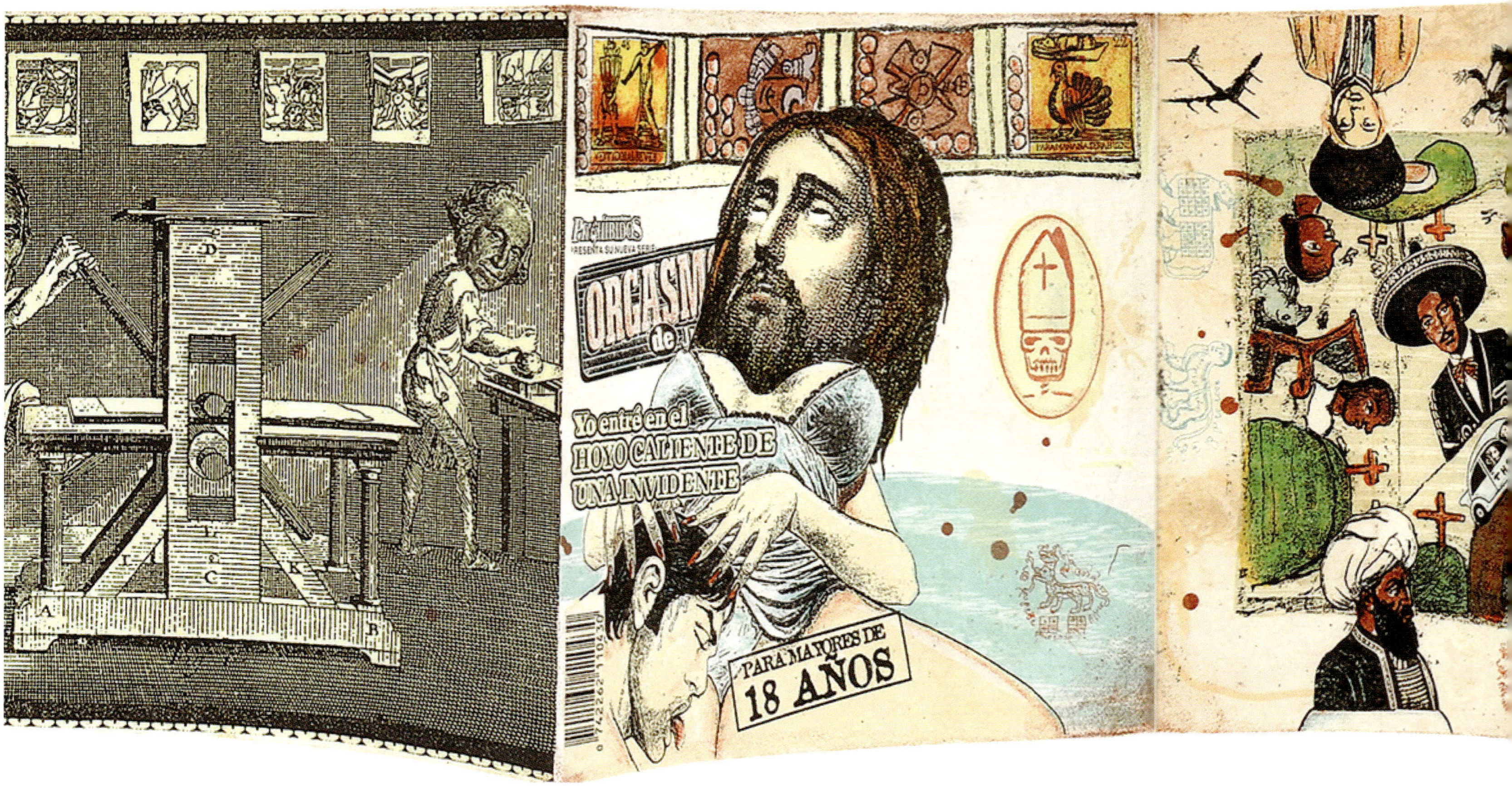
Yo entré en el
HOYO CALIENTE DE
UNA INVIDENTE
PARA MAYORES DE
18 AÑOS

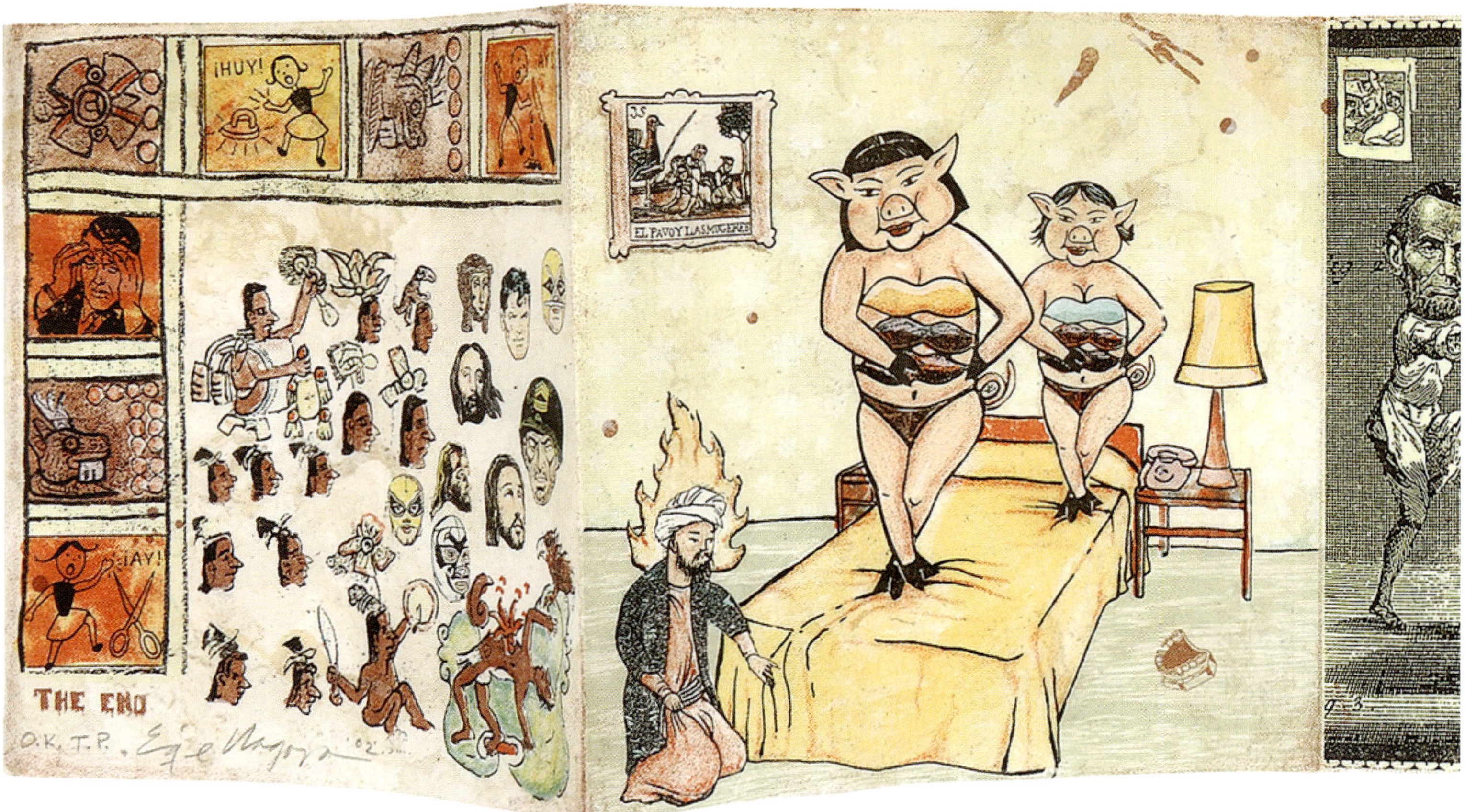

The Misadventures of the Romantic Cannibals

Texcoco was in the east of the city and was ruled by an architect/poet—King Netzahualcoyotl. King Neza organized poetry festivals and most importantly was against human sacrifices. He developed new concepts of God and cosmogony. He said that nobody had ever seen God so therefore he built temples with no sculpture to worship. It's a very modern concept to think of an abstract God, who does not look like us. King Neza developed that concept. He was an architect as well. One of the largest things he built was the giant library in Texcoco. This was like the Athens of the kingdom. It housed thousands and thousands of books on different topics from the historical origin of the Aztecs, as well as narratives about the cultures they conquered. There were also books on medicine. The Aztecs knew a lot about medicine. They were aware of penicillin, for example, which wasn't discovered by Europeans until the 1920s.

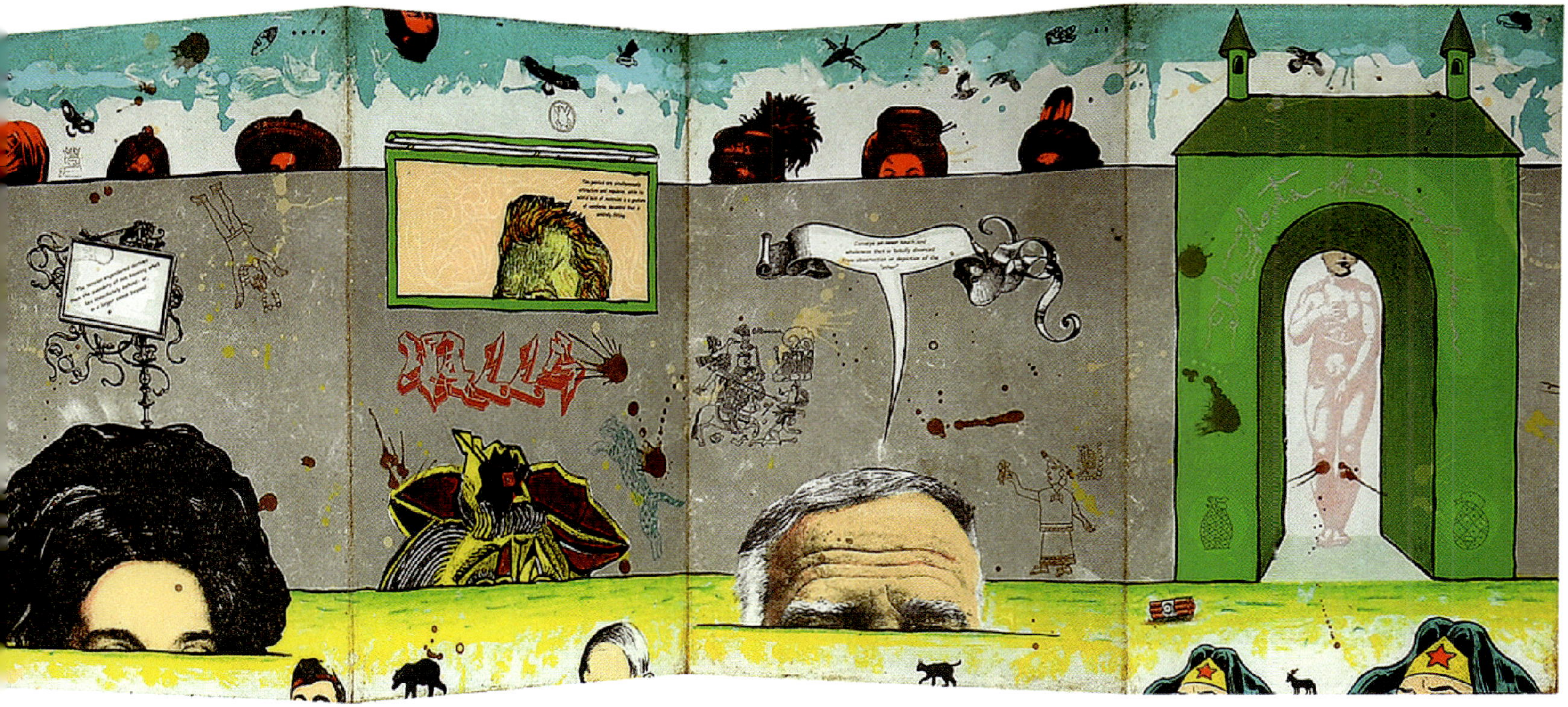

The Ghosts of Borderlandia, 2017

Color lithograph with chine collé. 15 x 80 in.

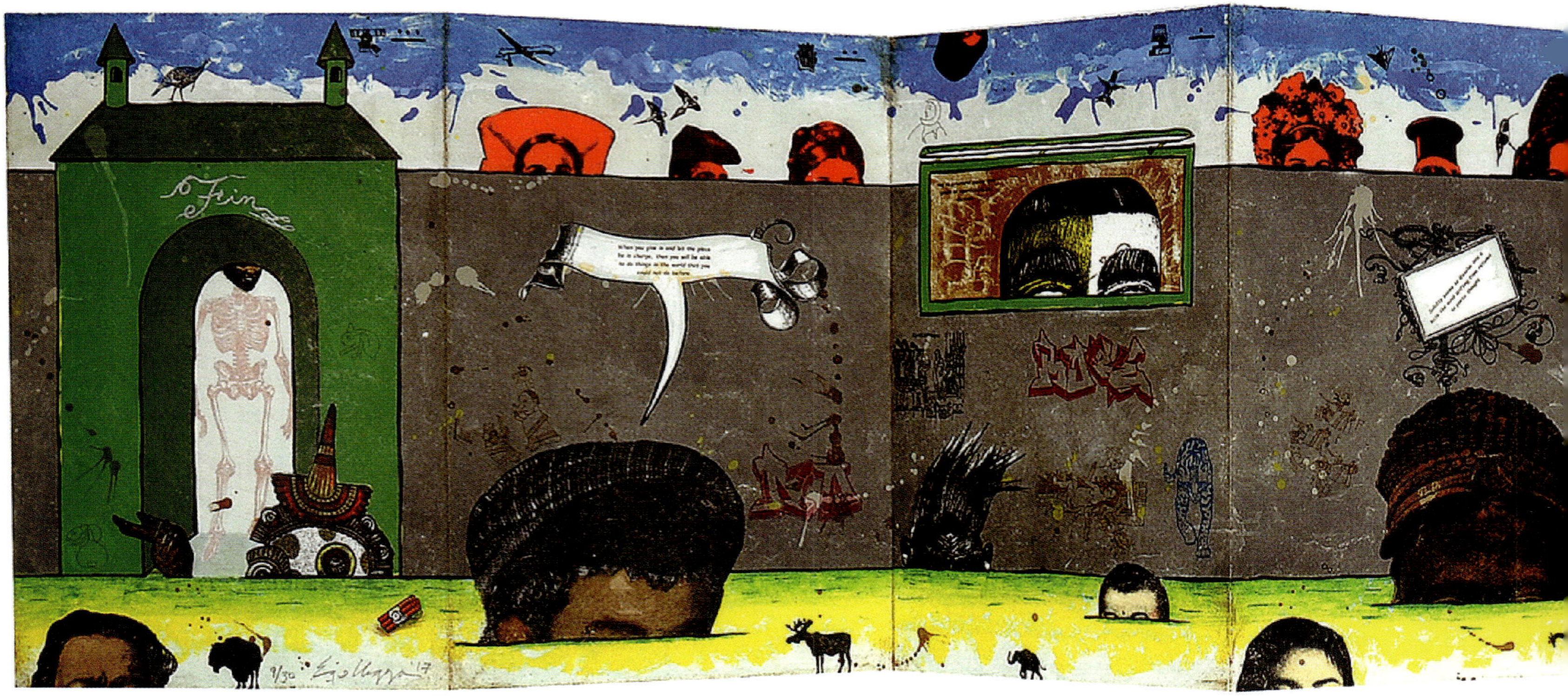
Fin

The library of Mexico City was 100% destroyed in 1521; that's when the conquest was over. The Spanish conquistadors and priests discovered the library and they decided that people were worshipping books and they piled them up in a bonfire and burnt them all. When the indigenous people witnessed the destruction of their library and the books, there was a mass suicide. The Spanish could not stop them. They hung themselves from trees, jumped off pyramids and killed themselves any way they could. An indigenous survivor, Fernando de Alva Ixtlilxochitl, whose name was Christianized, wrote this history. He was a noble Indian who survived the conquest and wrote these descriptions of King Nezahualcoyotl and the library in the Codex Ixtlilxochitl, with illustrations of King Nezahuatlcoyotl that I have used in my work.

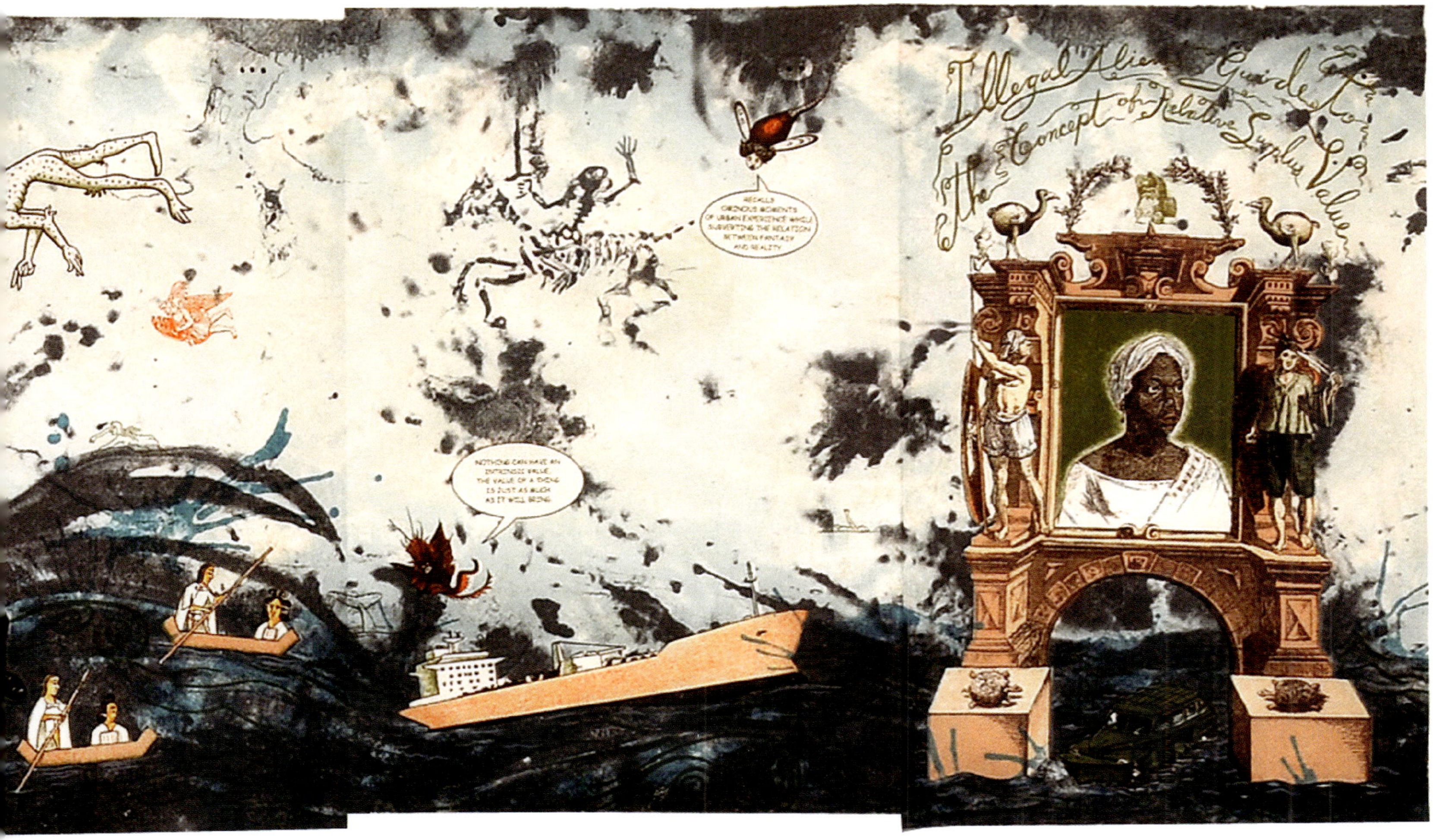

Illegal Alien's Guide to the Concept of Relative Surplus Value, 2009
Color lithograph. 15 x 80 in.

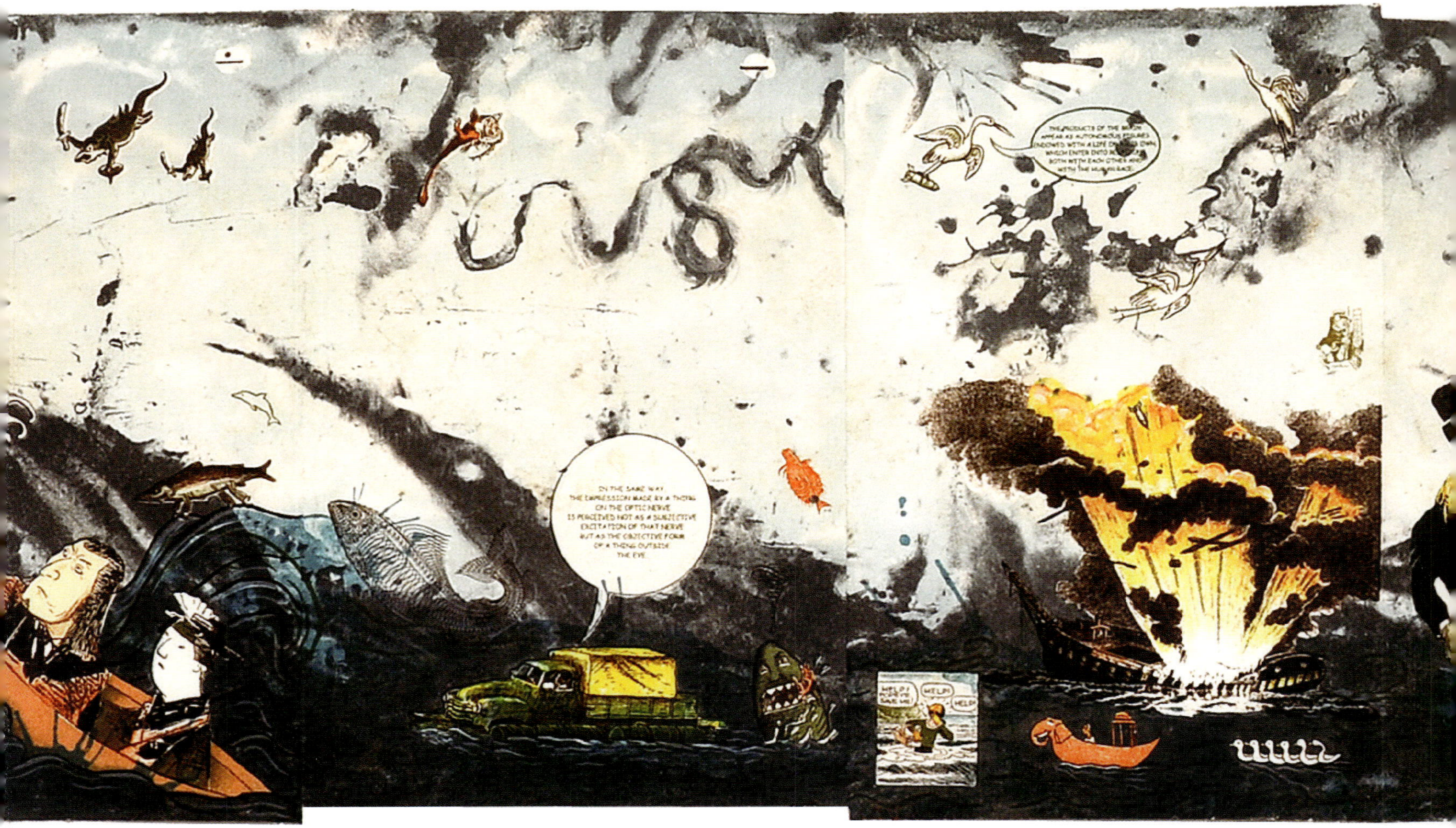
IN THE SAME WAY
THE IMPRESSION MADE BY A THING
ON THE OPTIC NERVE
IS PERCEIVED NOT AS A SUBJECTIVE
EXCITATION OF THAT NERVE
BUT AS THE OBJECTIVE FORM
OF A THING OUTSIDE
THE EYE
THE PRODUCTS OF THE BRAIN
APPEAR AS AUTONOMOUS FIGURES
BOTH WITH EACH OTHER AND
WITH THE HUMAN RACE
HELP!
HELP!

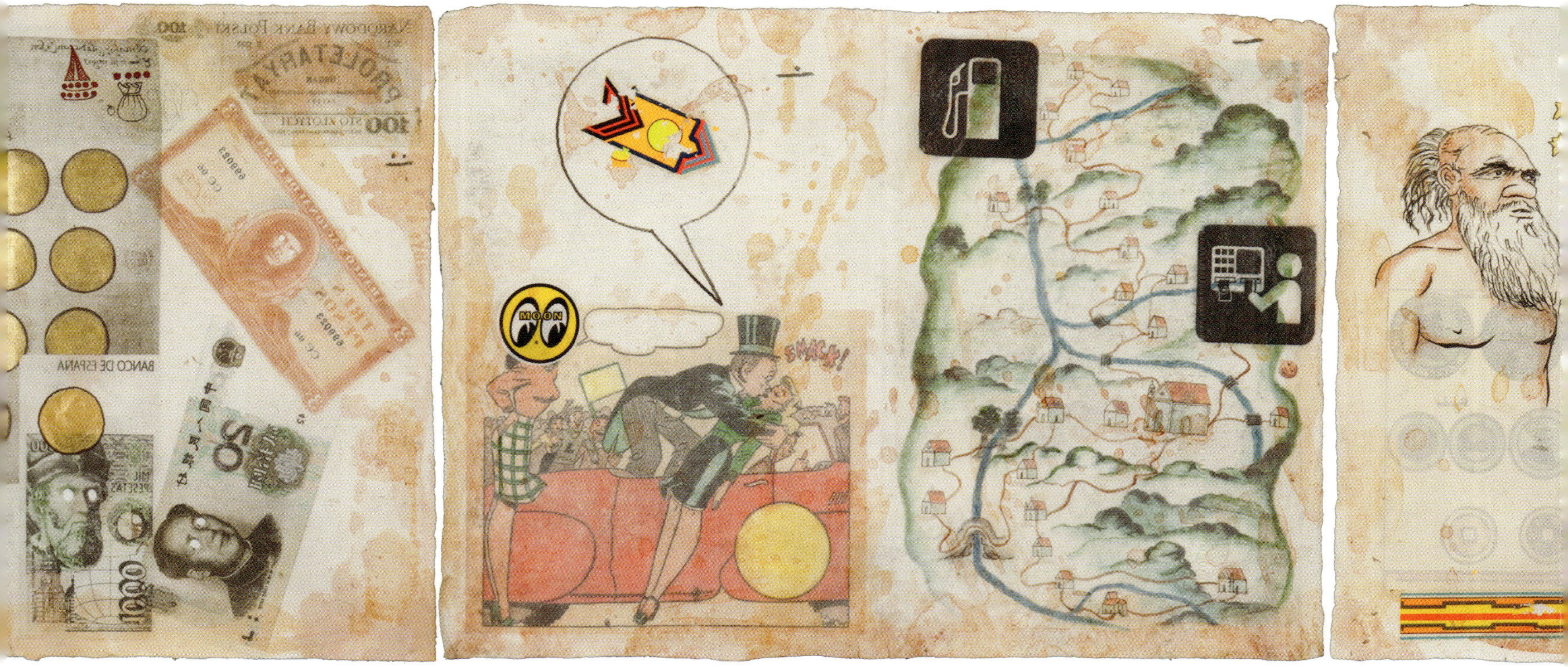
MOON
SMACK!

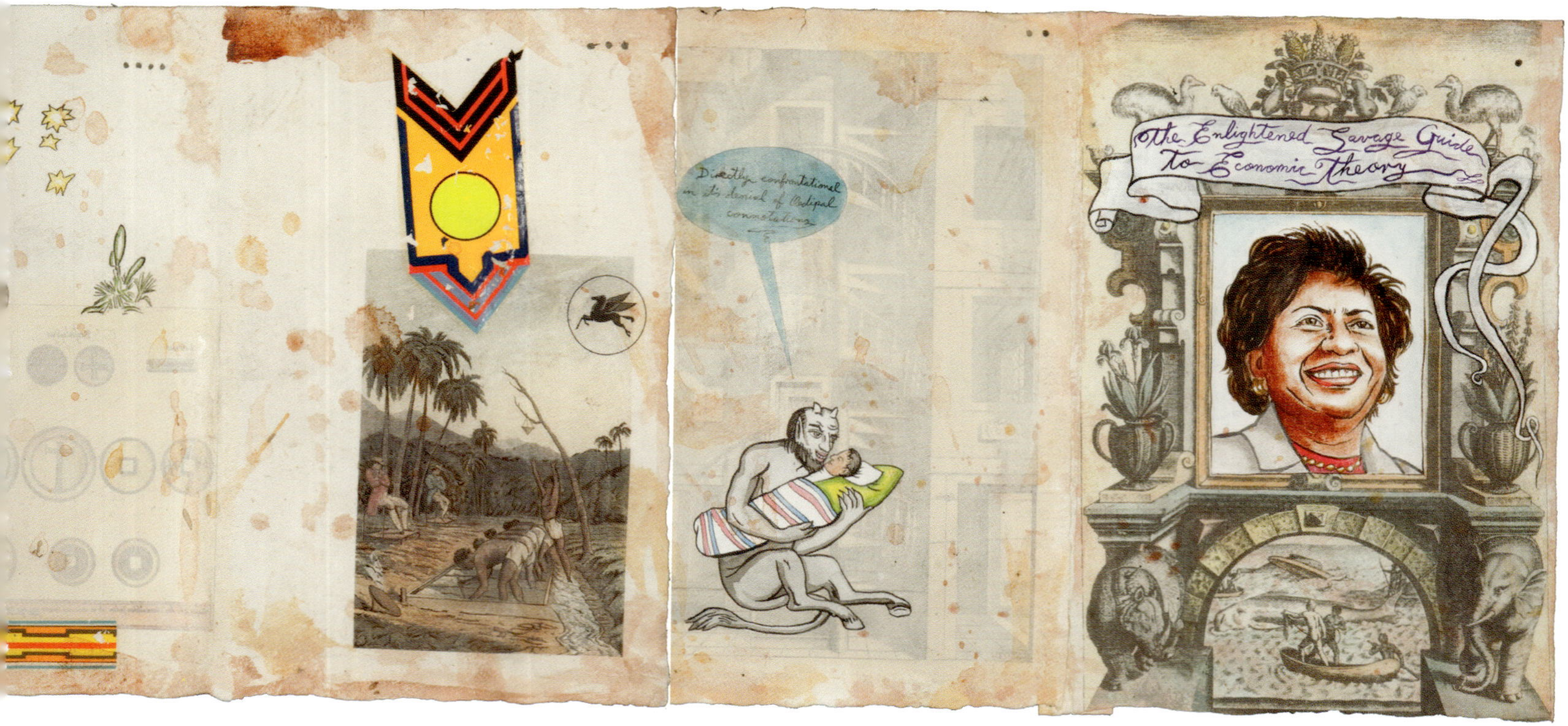

The Enlightened Savage Guide to Economic Theory, 2010
Acrylic, water based oil, solvent transfers and decals. 11 1/2 x 108 1/2 in.

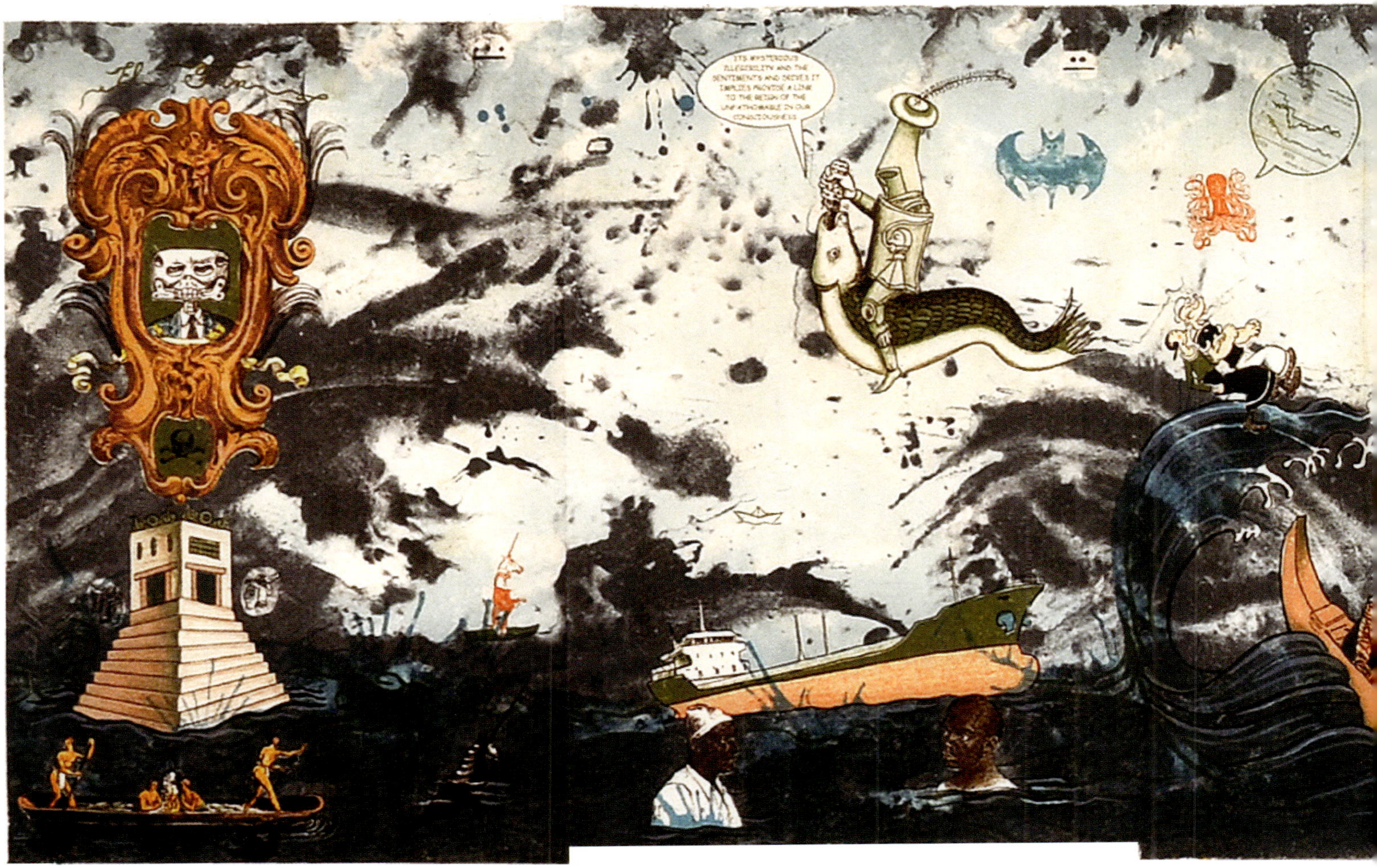

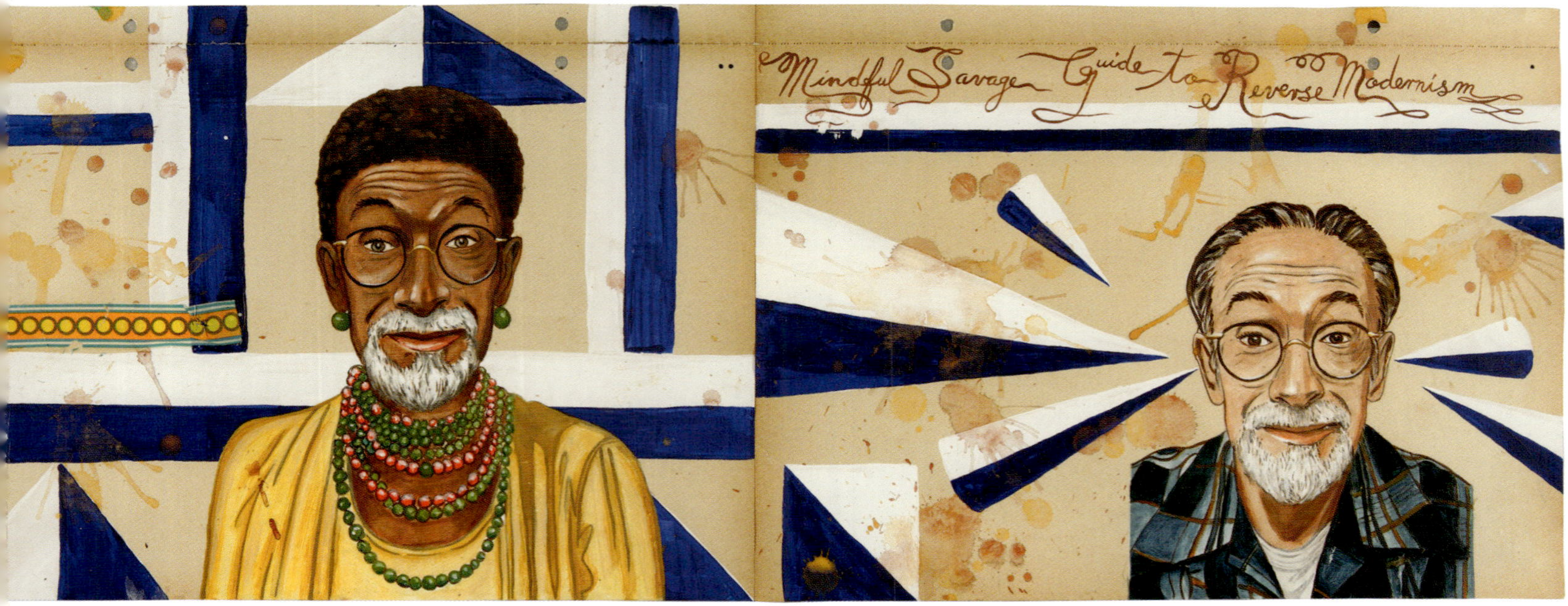

Mindful Savage Guide to Reverse Modernism, 2016
Acrylic and water based oil on de-acidified vintage paper. 11 x 96 in.

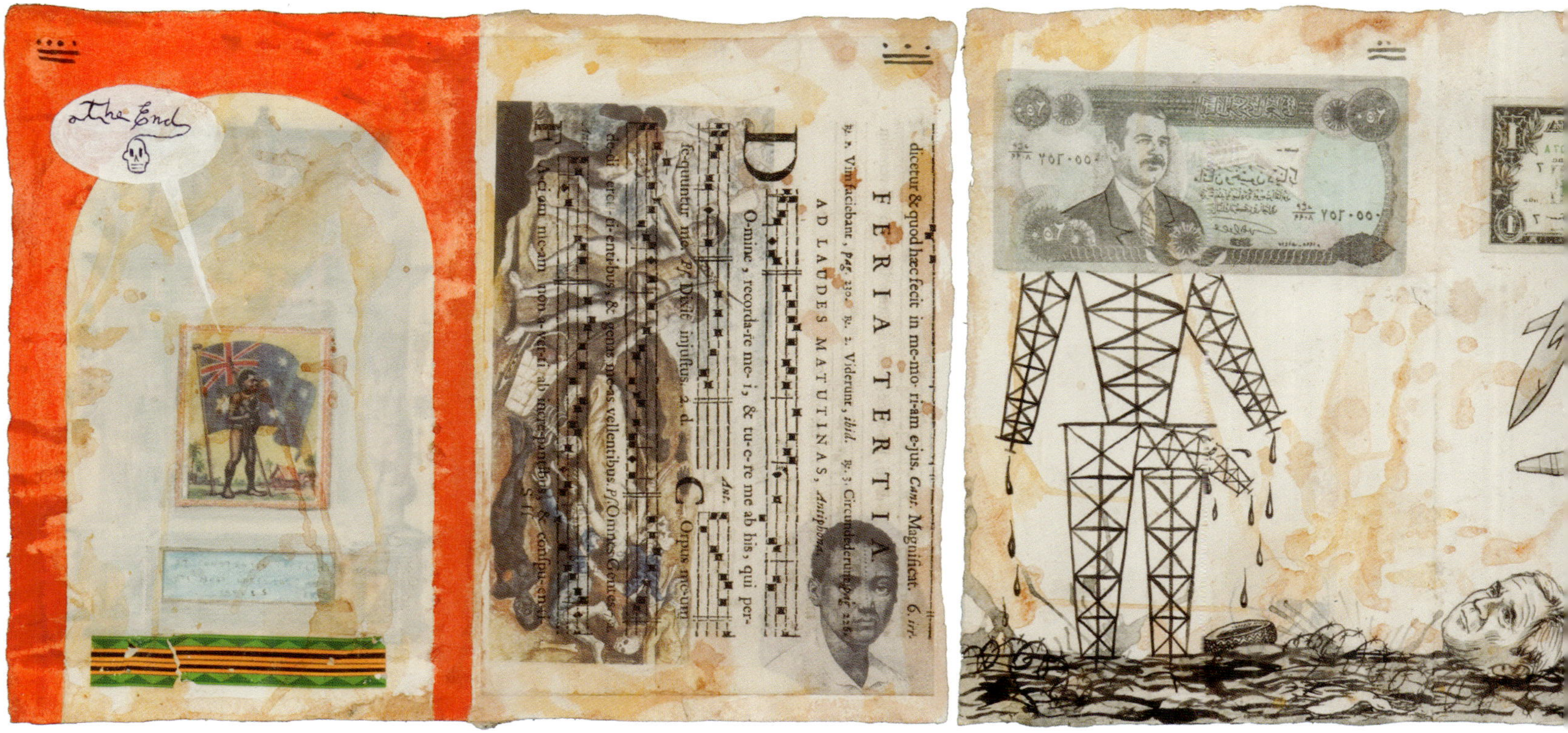

the End

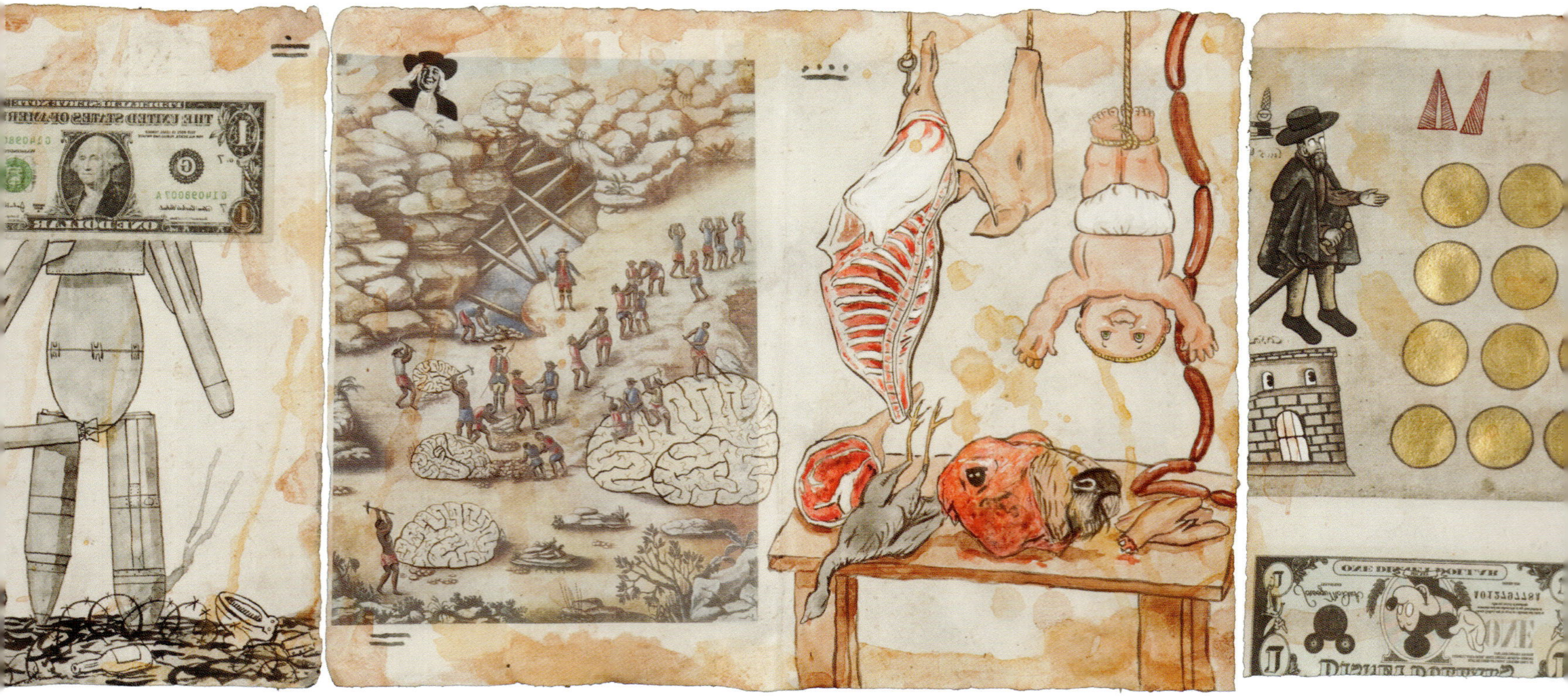

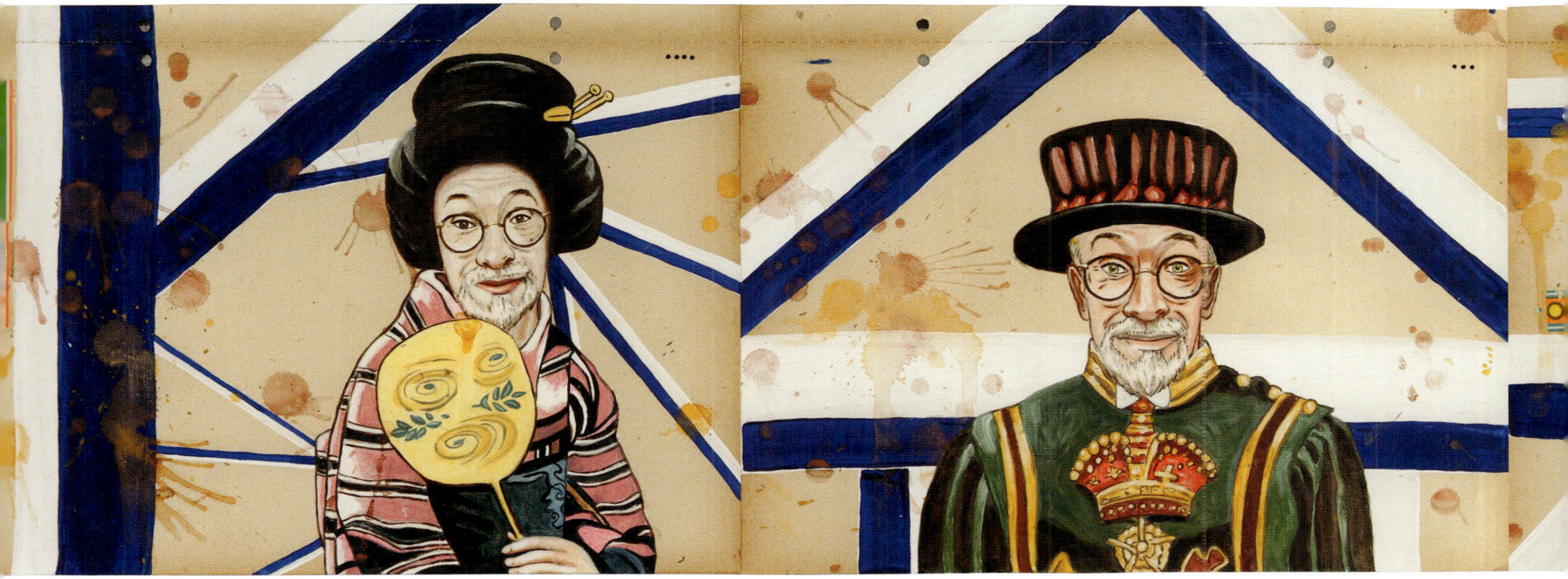

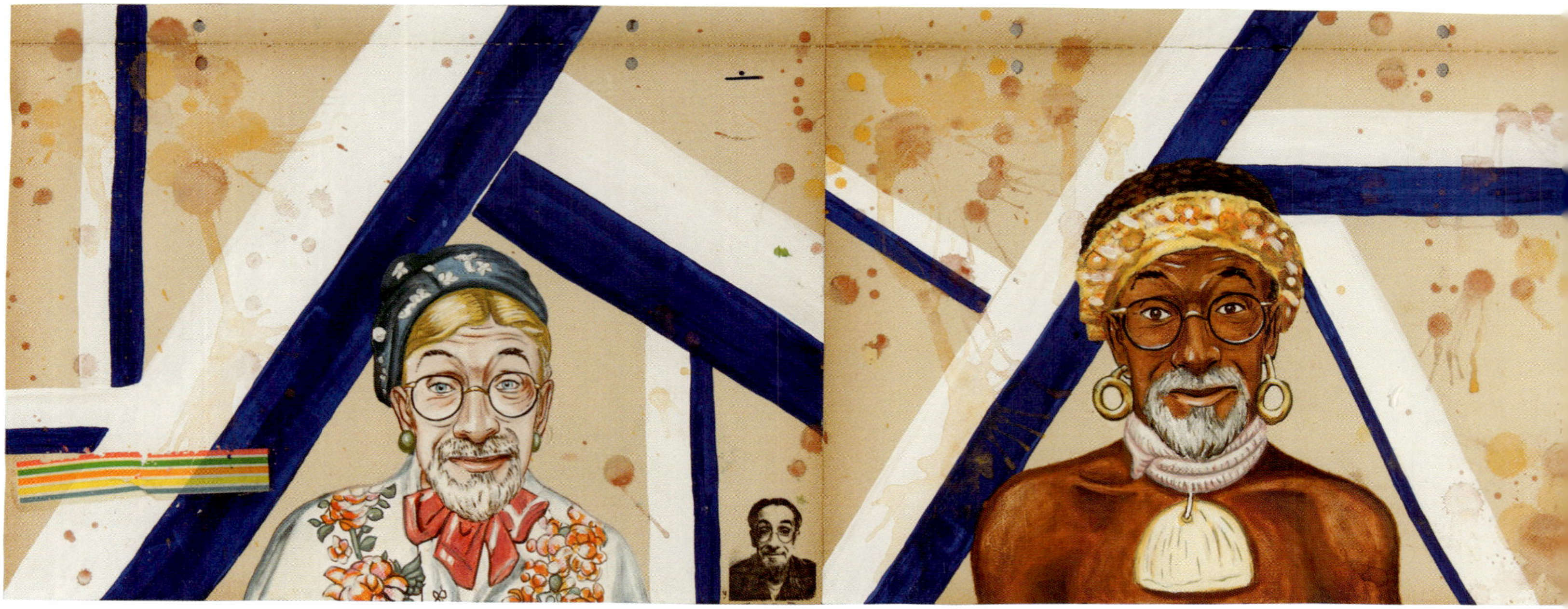

The Mayan codices had a similar fate. Only three Mayan codices survive: the Codex Madrid in Spain, the Codex Paris in France and the Codex Dresden in Germany. There is possibly one more in Mexico City with fragments of a Mayan book, but I am not sure if it is a hoax or for real. In addition to the Codex Ixtlilxochitl, completed soon after the conquest, a twelve-volume work by Fray Bernardino de Sahagún exists. He was a Spanish priest who interviewed indigenous people, asking them about their customs, Aztec history and religion. The twelve volumes were illustrated by indigenous artists but included European writing and followed something closer to Renaissance perspective than the pre-Columbian style, which is based completely on visual language with hardly any words. Pre-Columbian writing was not phonetic but visual.

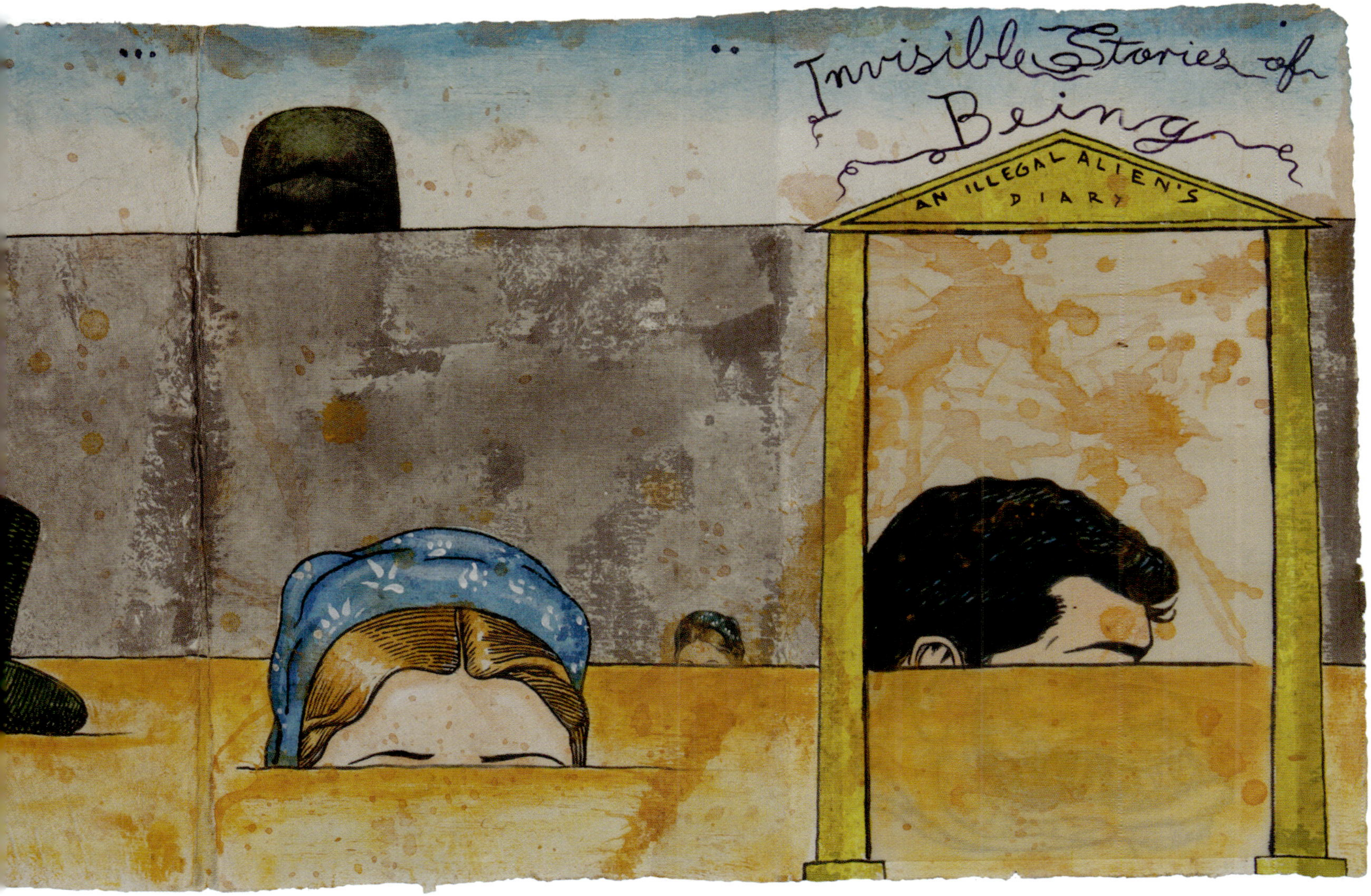

Invisible Stories of Being/An Illegal Alien's Diary, 2013
Acrylic, water based oil solvent transfers, decals and wood on handmade Amate paper. 12 x 107 1/2 in.

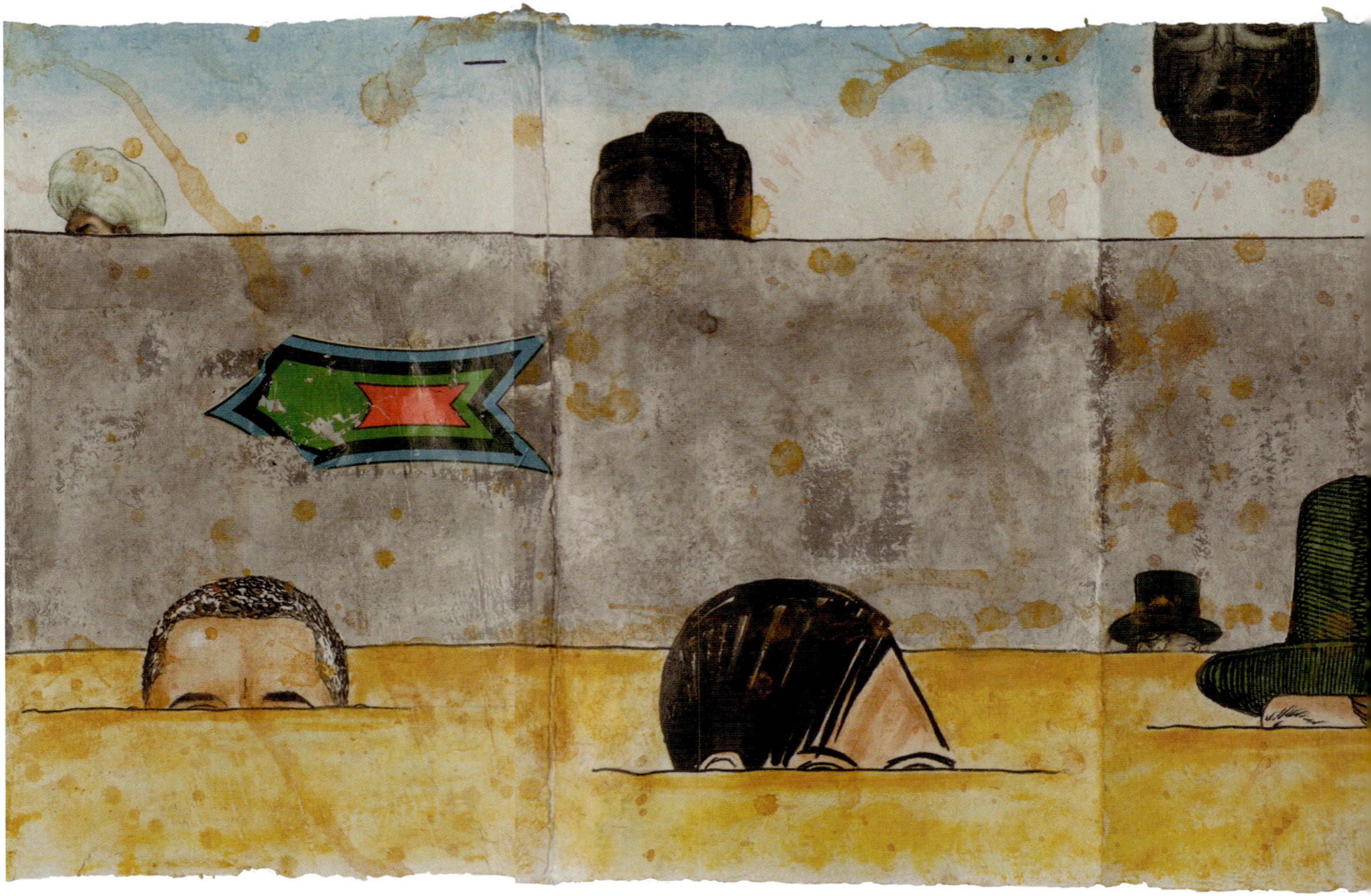

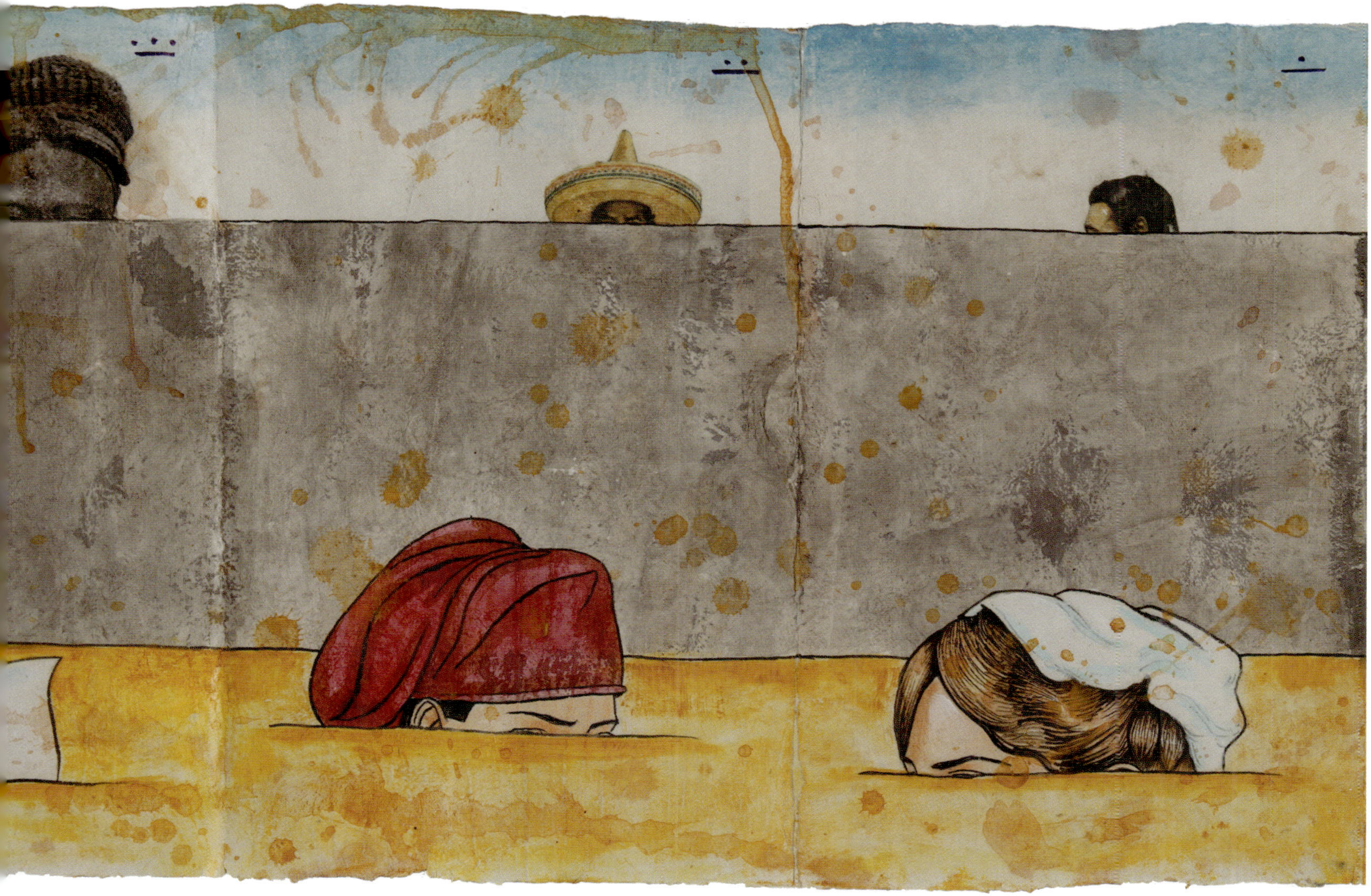

Invisible Stories of Being/An Illegal Alien's Diary

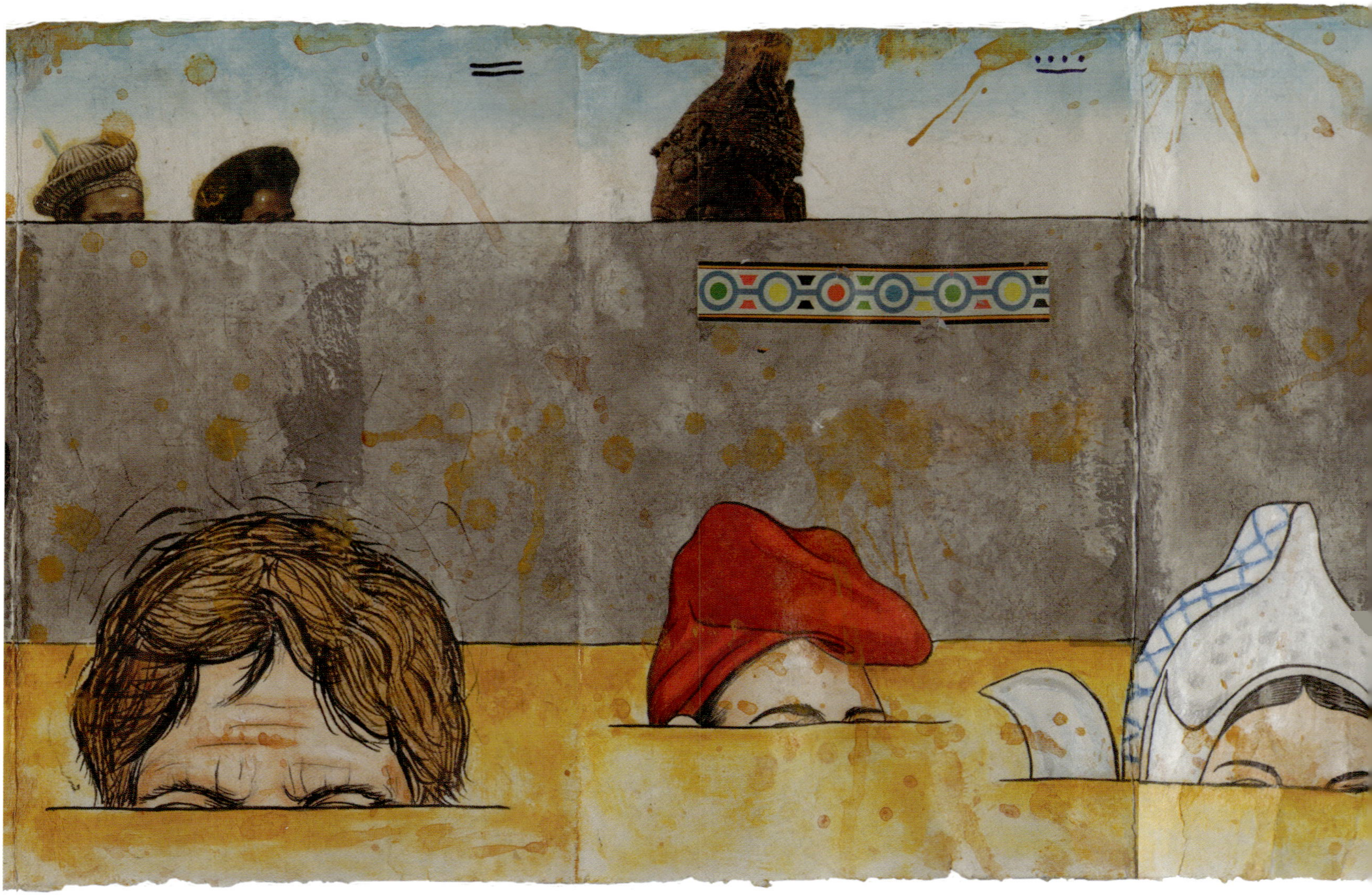

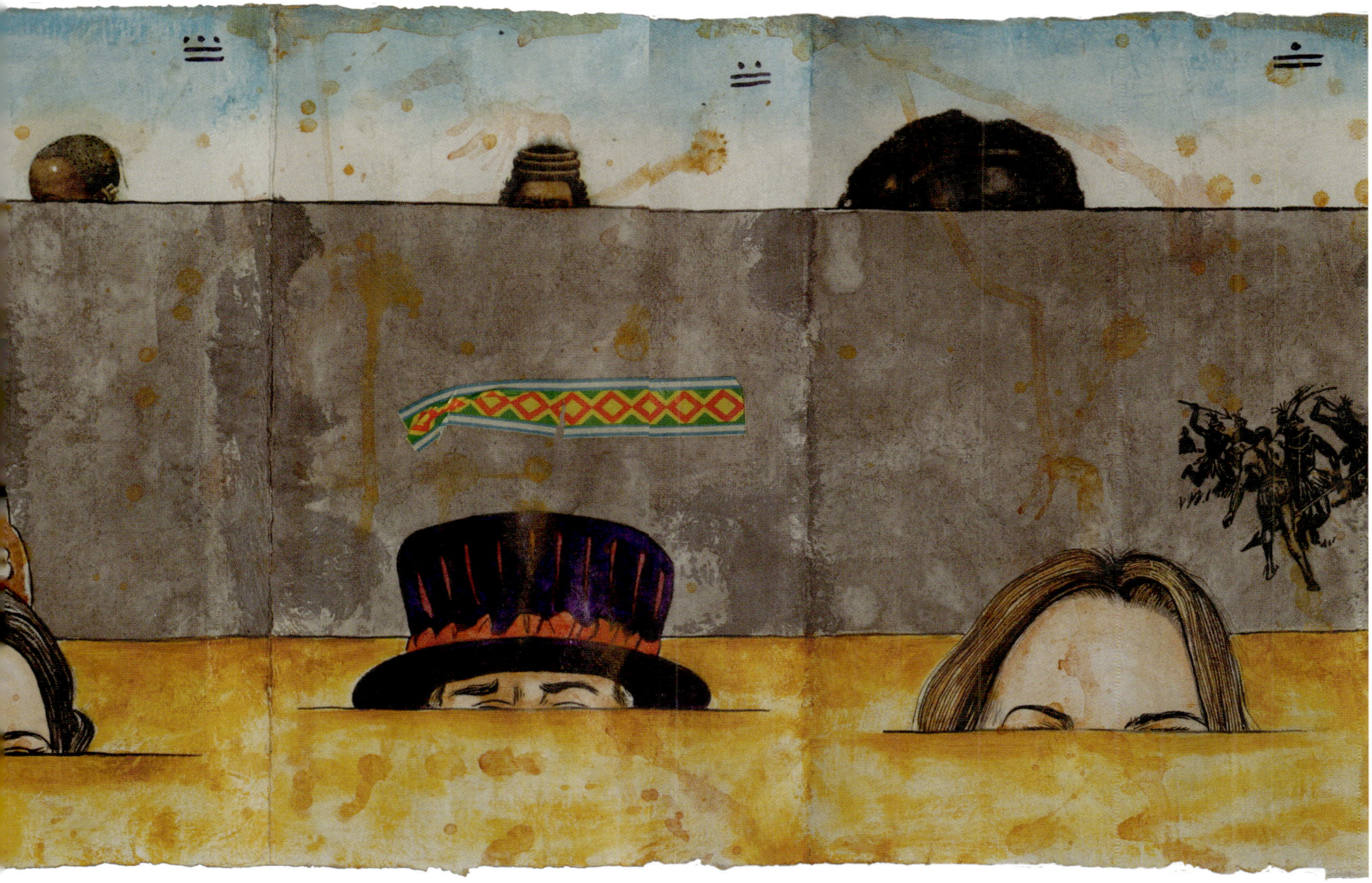

Invisible Stories of Being/An Illegal Alien's Diary

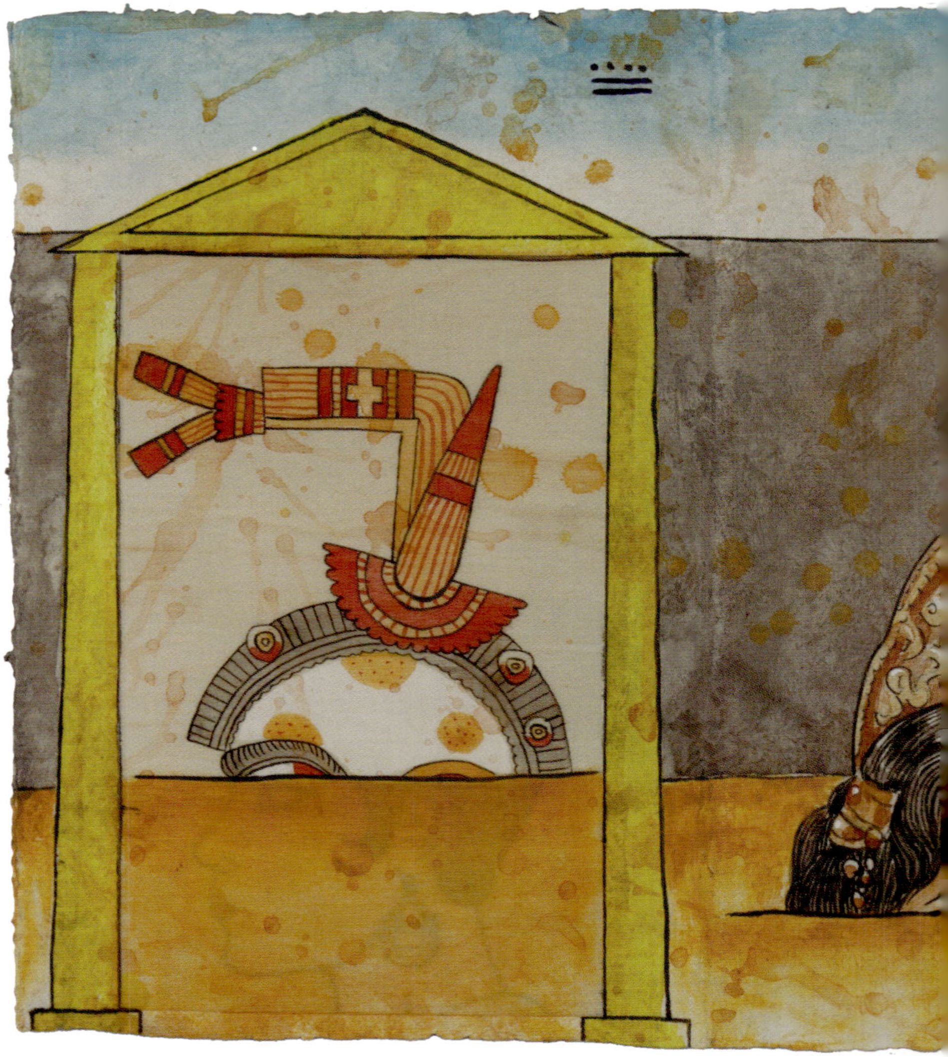

41-B

A single priest, Diego de Landa, is responsible for the destruction of all the Mayan books except for the three I mentioned. Everywhere he went in the Yucatán peninsula and in Guatemala he burnt Mayan books. The same thing happened to the Mixtec Zapotec books in Oaxaca. Only about nineteen of their books survived, so altogether there are only twenty-two pre-Columbian books—three Mayan and nineteen Mixtec Zapotec—no Aztec books except codices made after the conquest. For me, besides being a genocide, the conquest was a culturicide. According to the U.N., in the hundred years after the conquest the indigenous population diminished by 90% throughout the continent. I have not seen the statistics for this country, but I imagine they are similar.

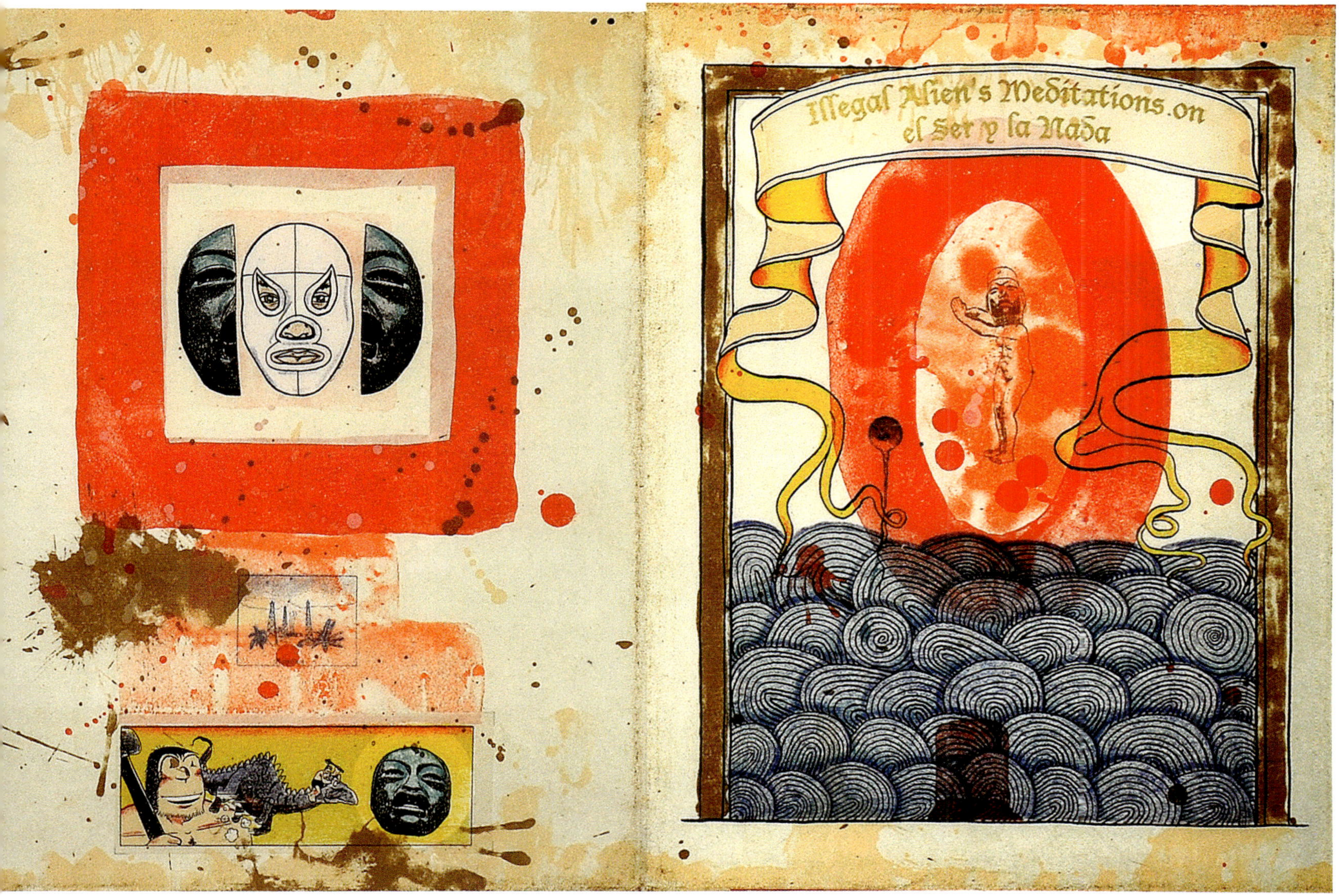

Illegal Alien's Meditations on el Ser y la Nada, 2012
Color lithograph with chine collé and gold powder. 14 x 88 in.

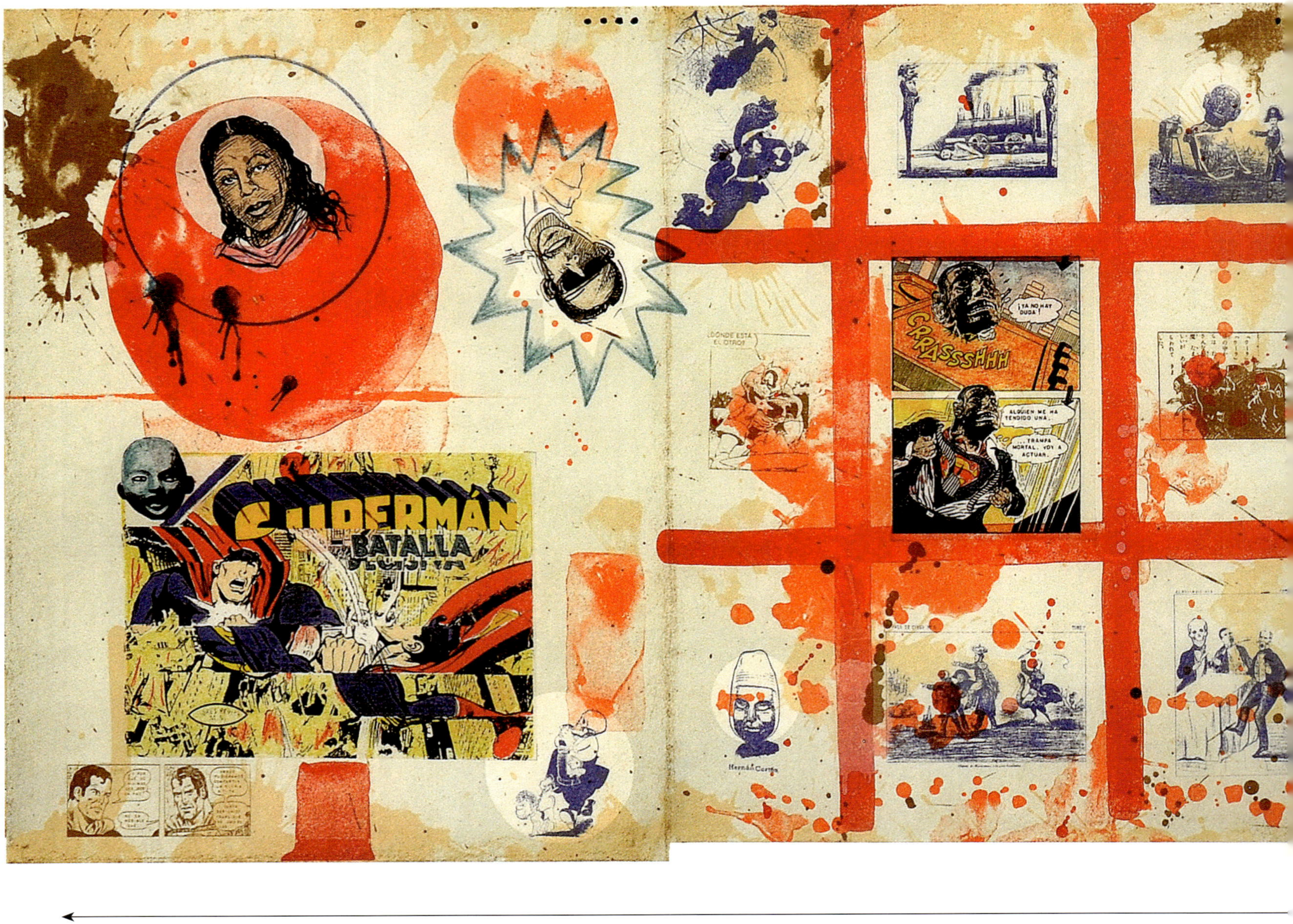
SUPERMÁN
BATALLA
¿DONDE ESTA EL OTRO?
¡YA NO HAY DUDA!
CRASSSHHH
ALGUIEN ME HA TENDIDO UNA...
...TRAMPA MORTAL. VOY A ACTUAR.
Hernán Cortés

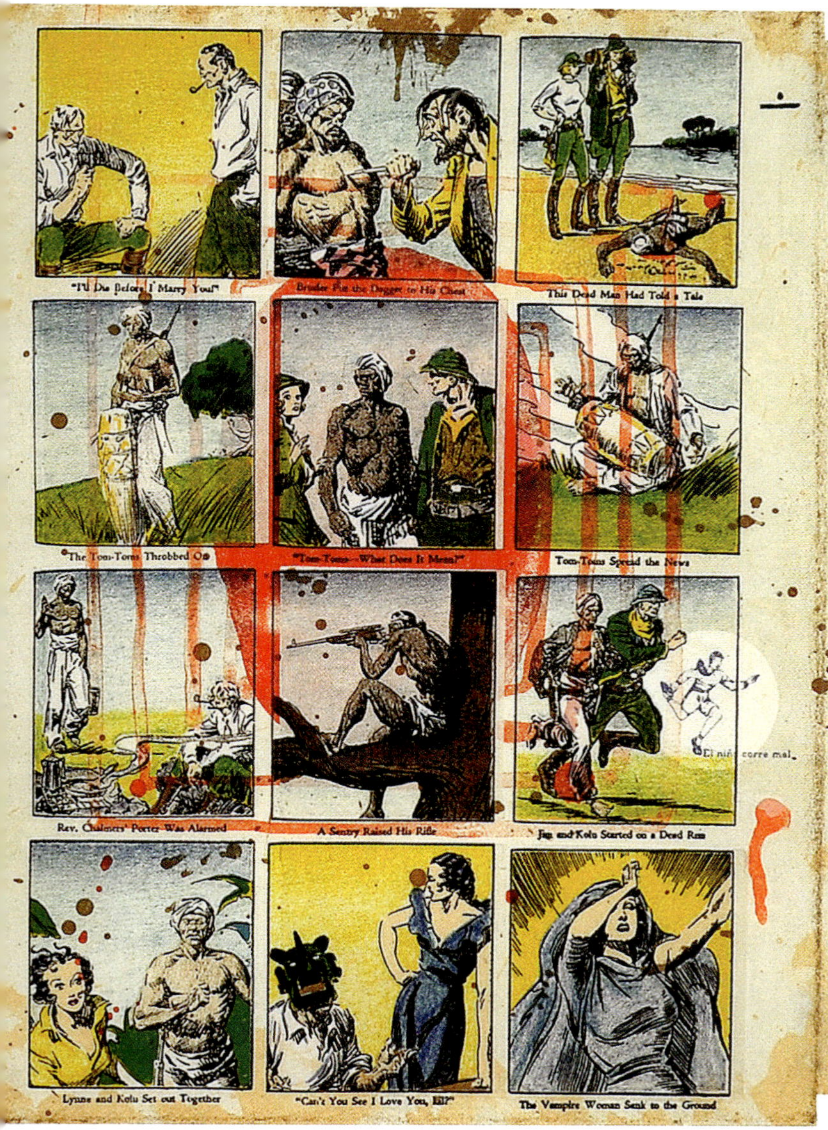

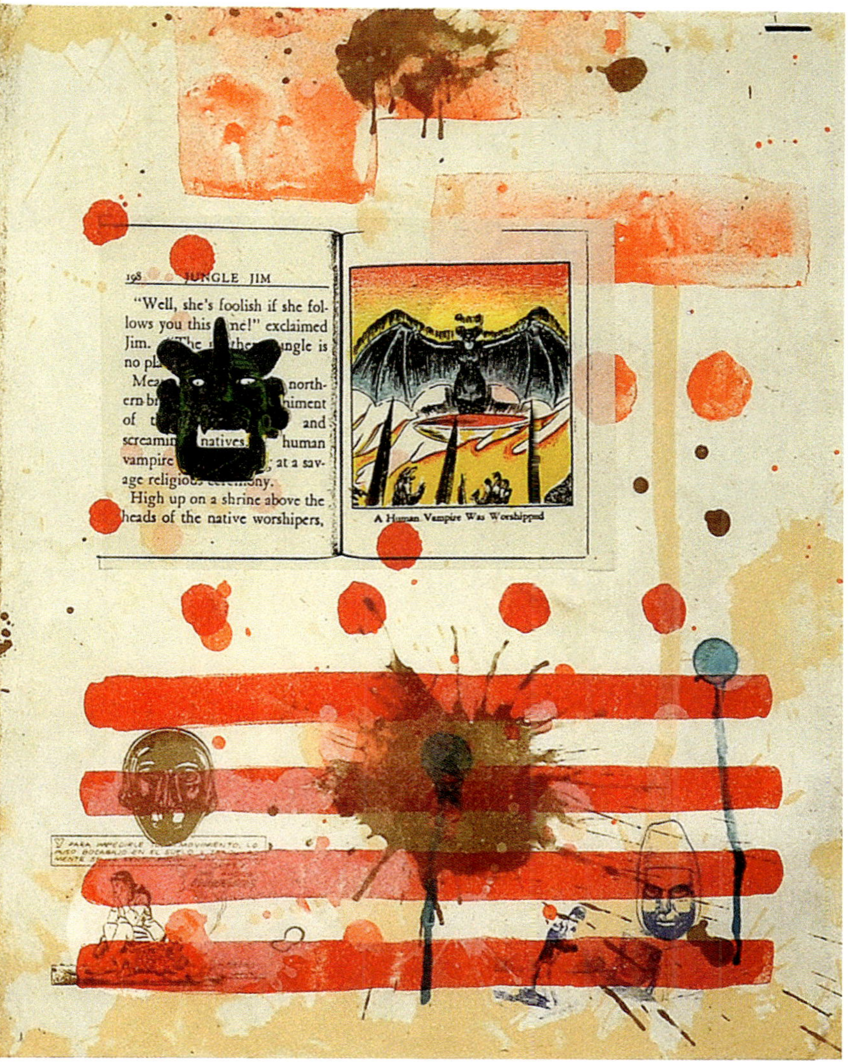

Illegal Alien's Meditations on el Ser y la Nada

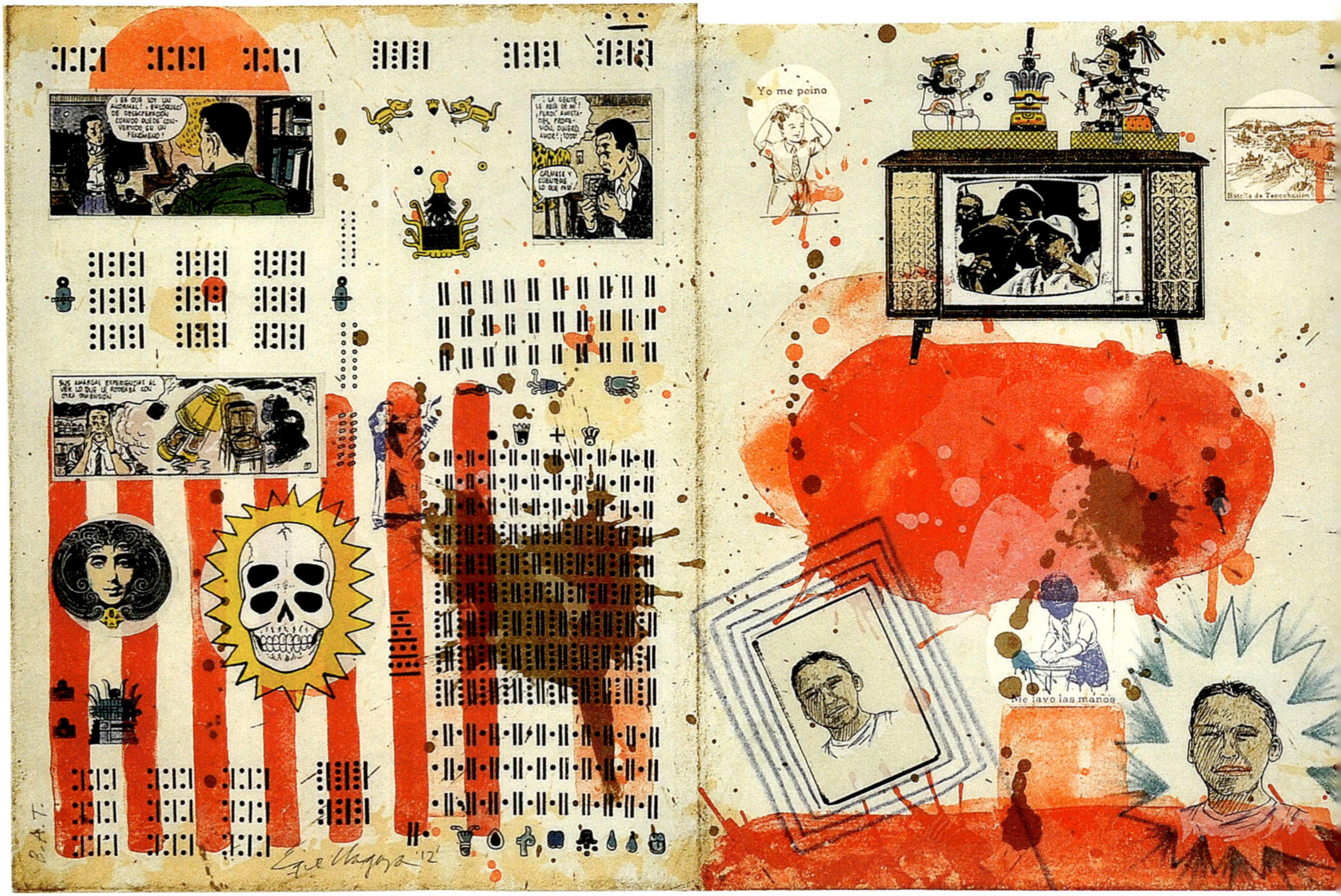
CALMESE Y CUENTEME LO QUE PASO
Yo me peino
Me lavo las manos
B.A.T.

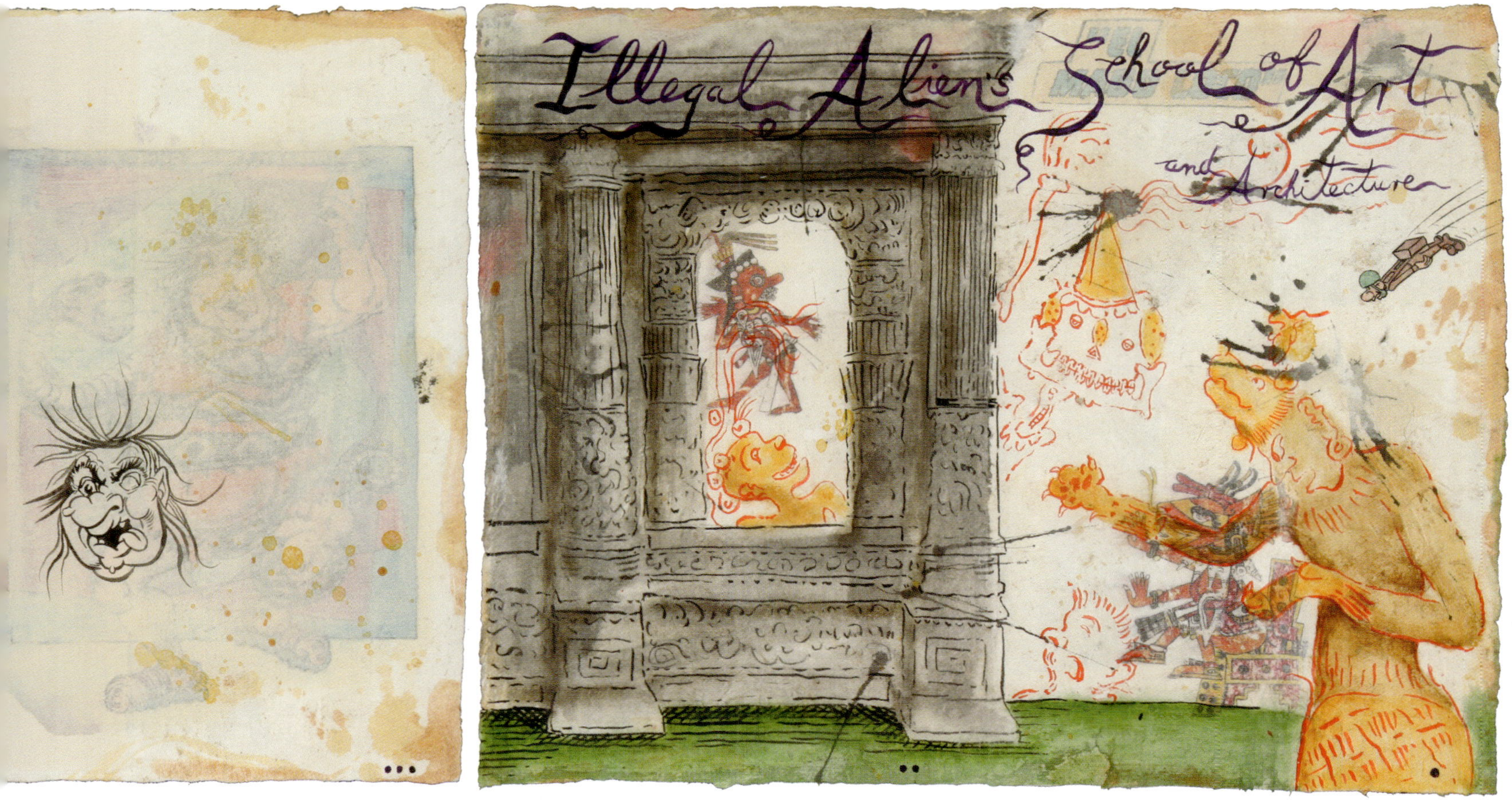

Illegal Alien's School of Art and Architecture, 2006

Acrylic, water based oil, solvent transfers and wood. 11 1/2 x 108 1/2 in.

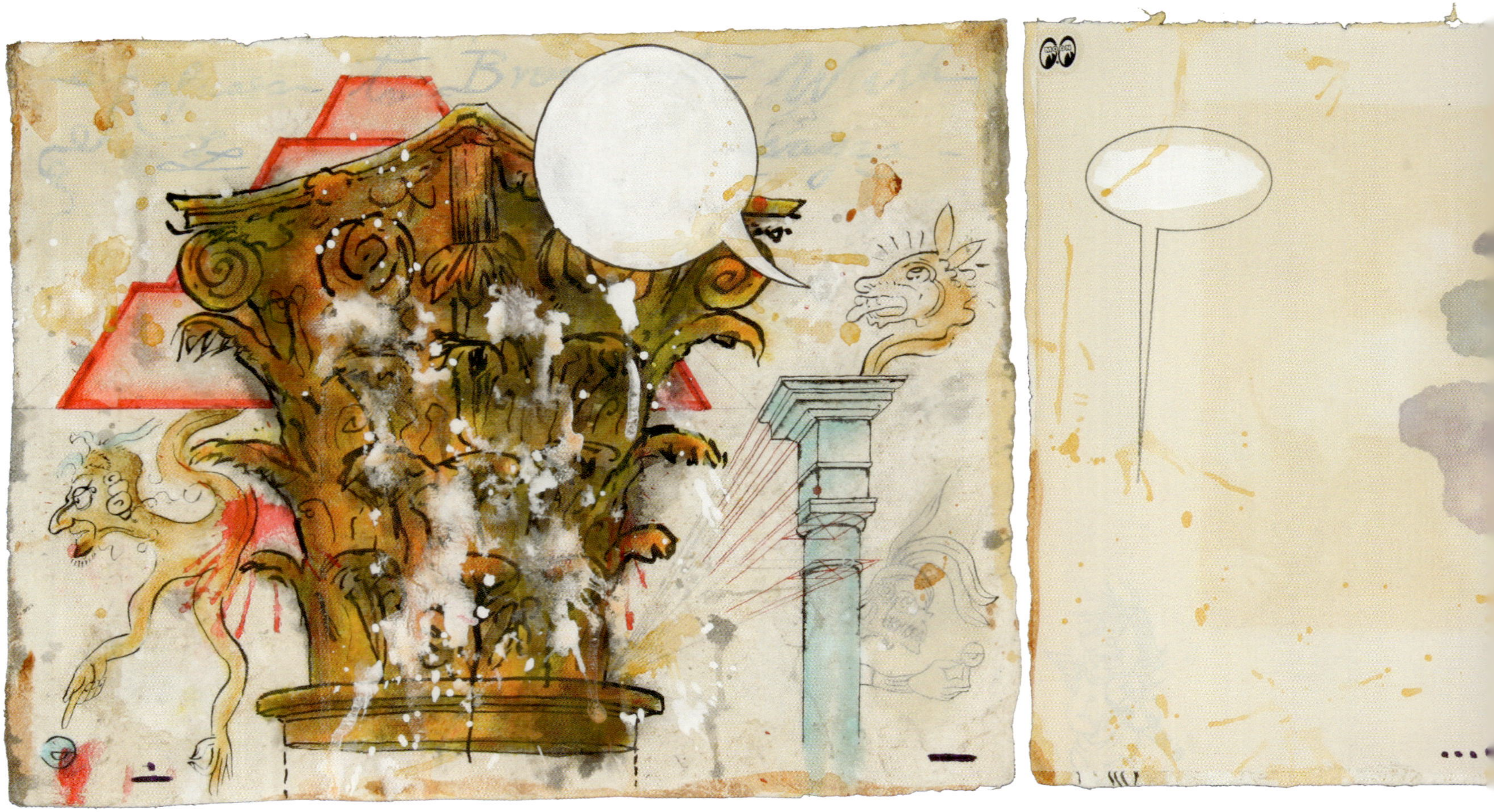

49-B

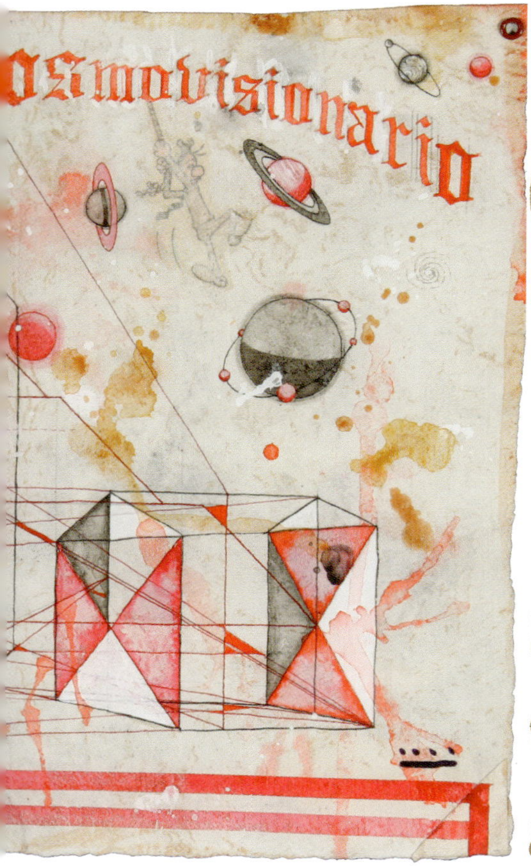

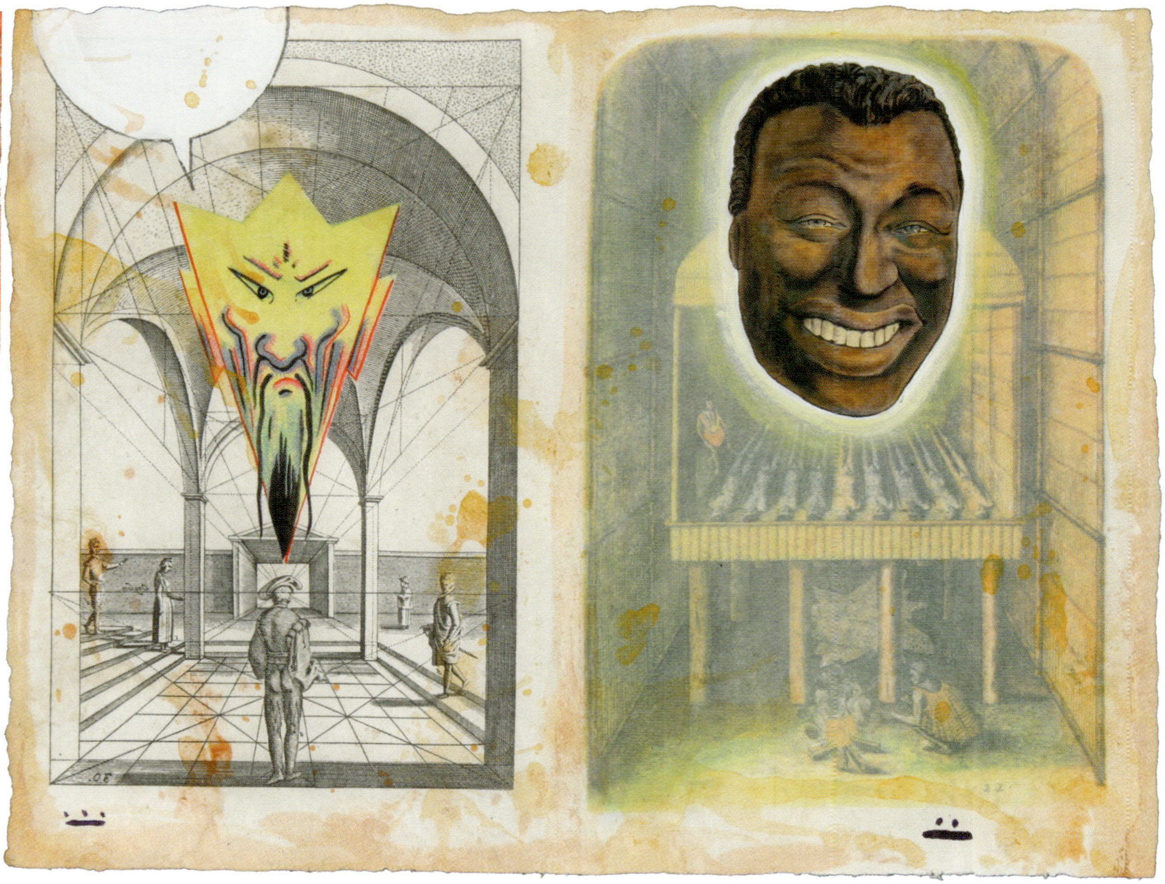

Illegal Alien's School of Art and Architecture

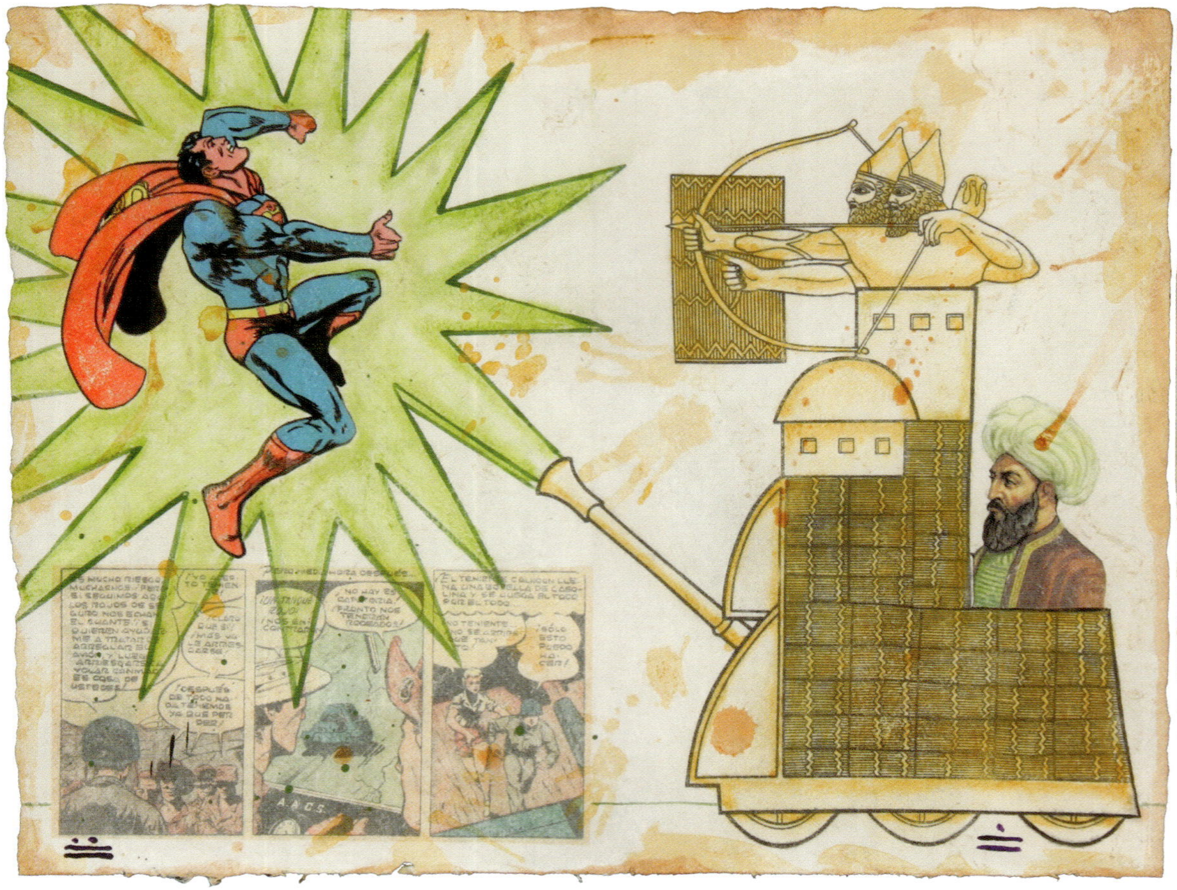
¡PRONTO NOS TENDRÁN RODEADOS!
¡DESPUÉS DE TODO NADA TENEMOS YA QUE PERDER!
¡SÓLO ESTO PUEDO HACER!

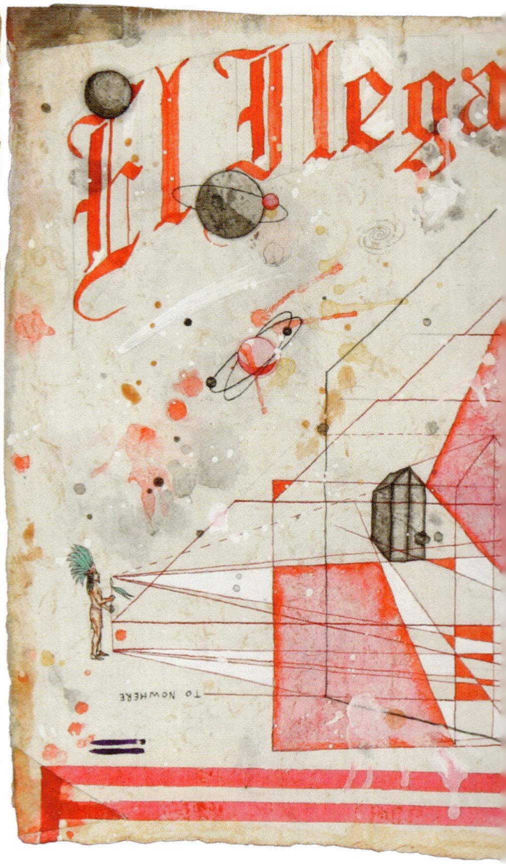
El Ilega
TO NOWHERE

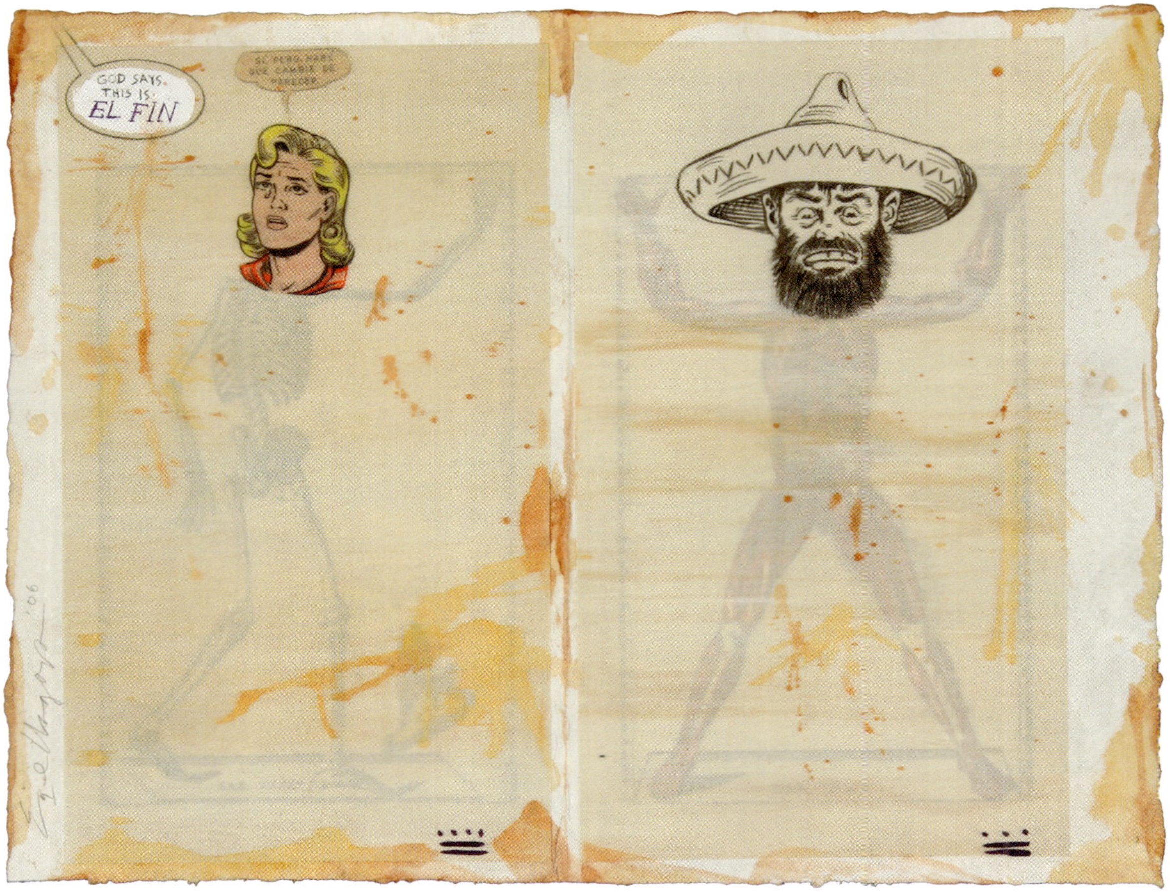

Illegal Alien's School of Art and Architecture

Those who win the wars write history; that includes the Aztecs who burnt books of cultures they conquered. History written by the victors is an ideological construction more than a science. So I decided that as an artist I have the right to make my own construction of history, not necessarily ideological but by using artistic license to construct a narrative, with humor and a more contemporary feel, that is different from the dominant history. I began to do my codices based on the history I learnt and I pretended to be an indigenous artist who traveled through time making codices and creating similar visual language.

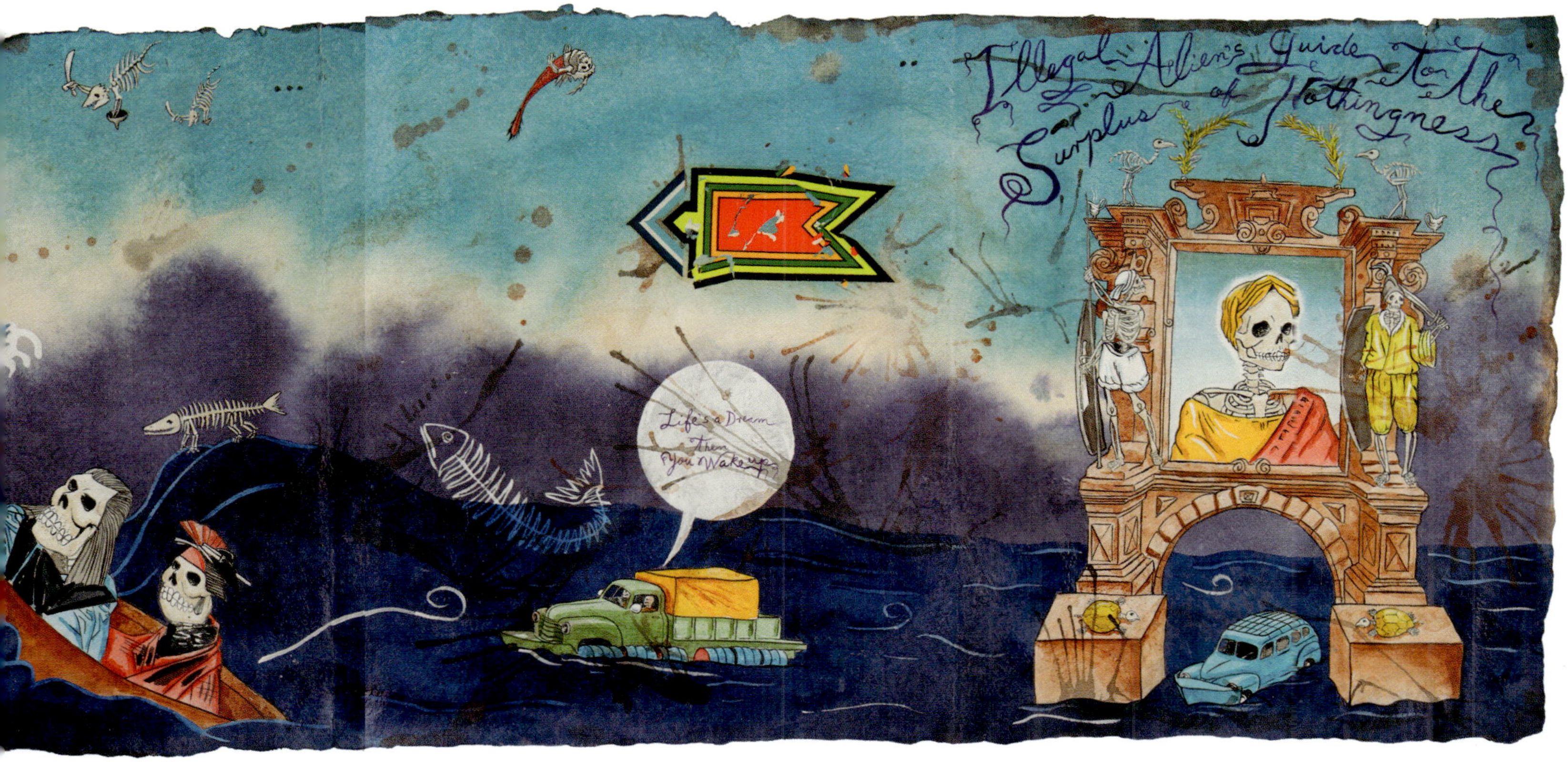

Illegal Alien's Guide to the Surplus of Nothingness, 2009
Acrylic, water based oil and decals. 12 x 82 in.

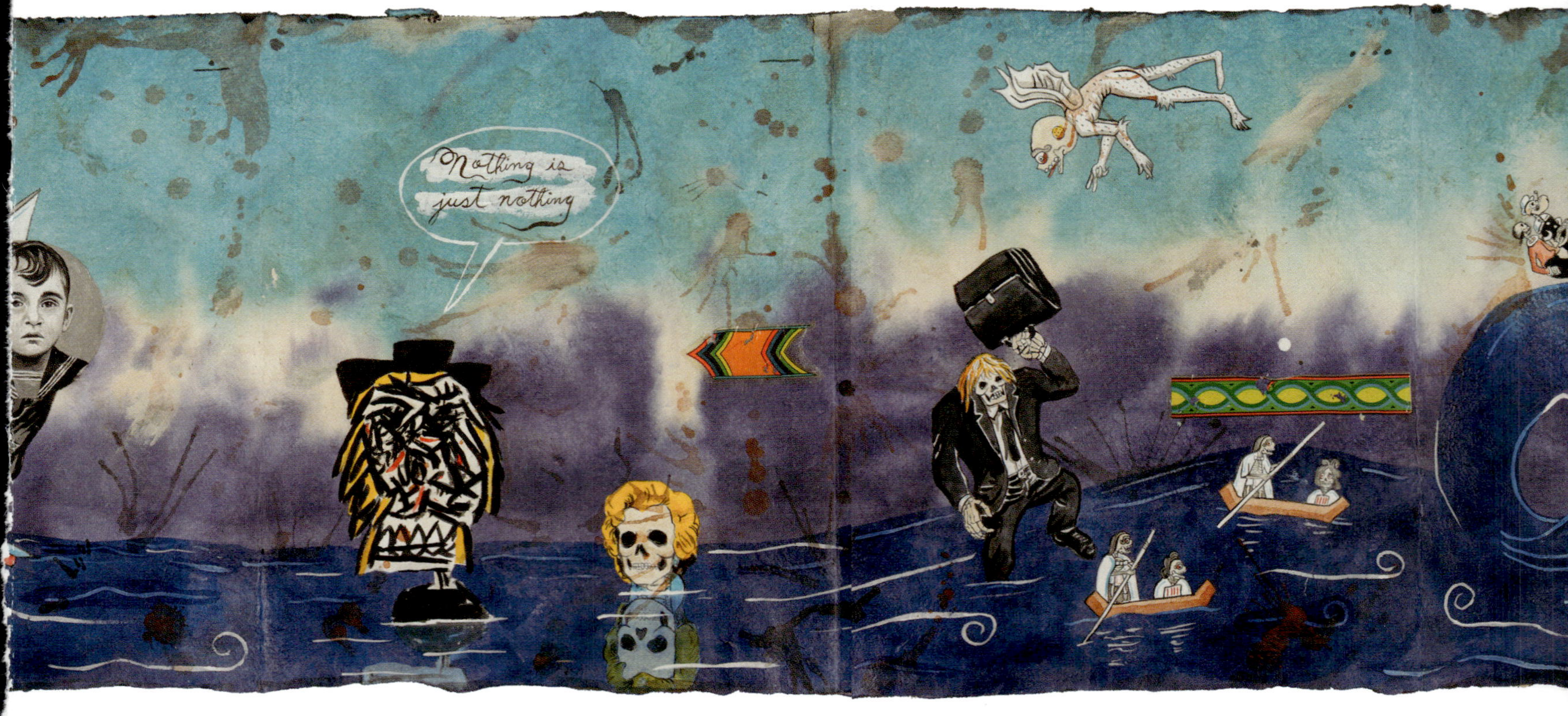
Nothing is
just nothing

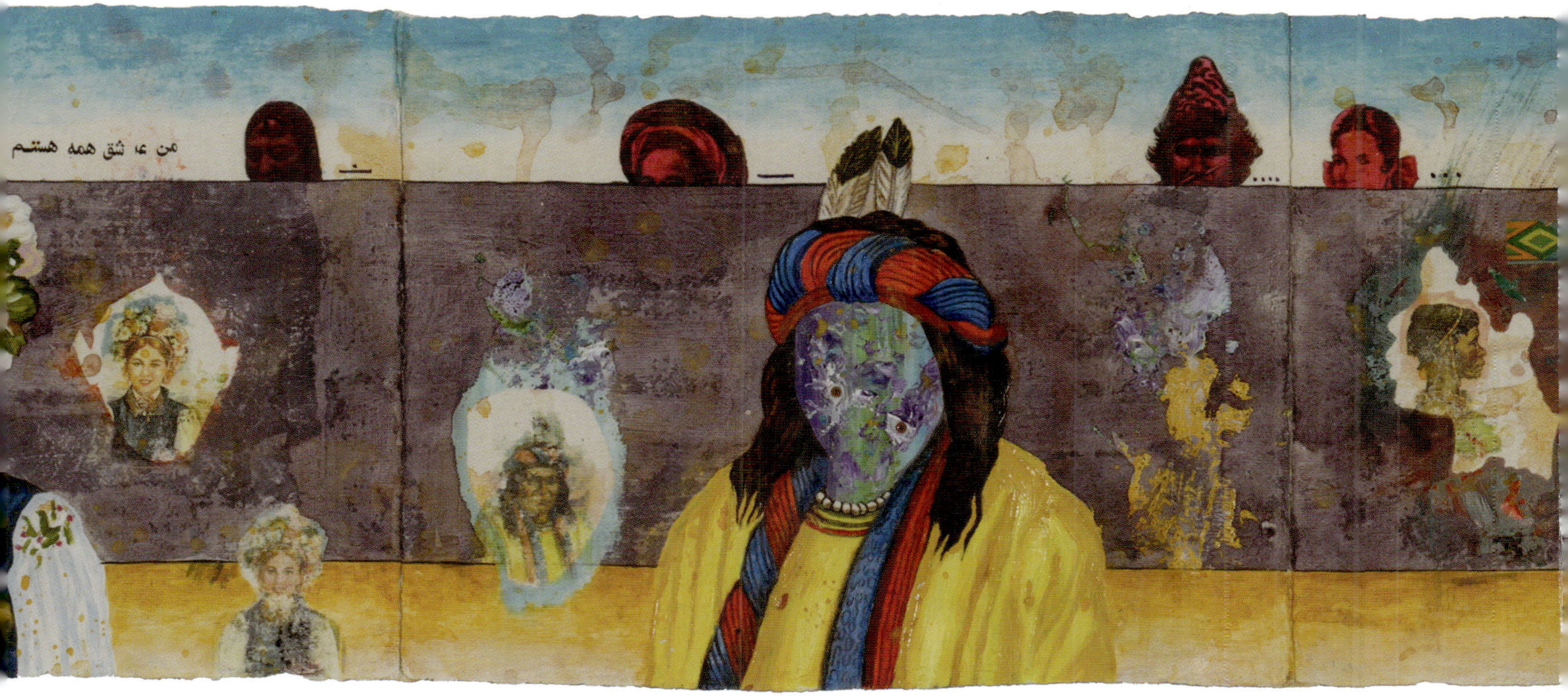
من عاشق همه هستم

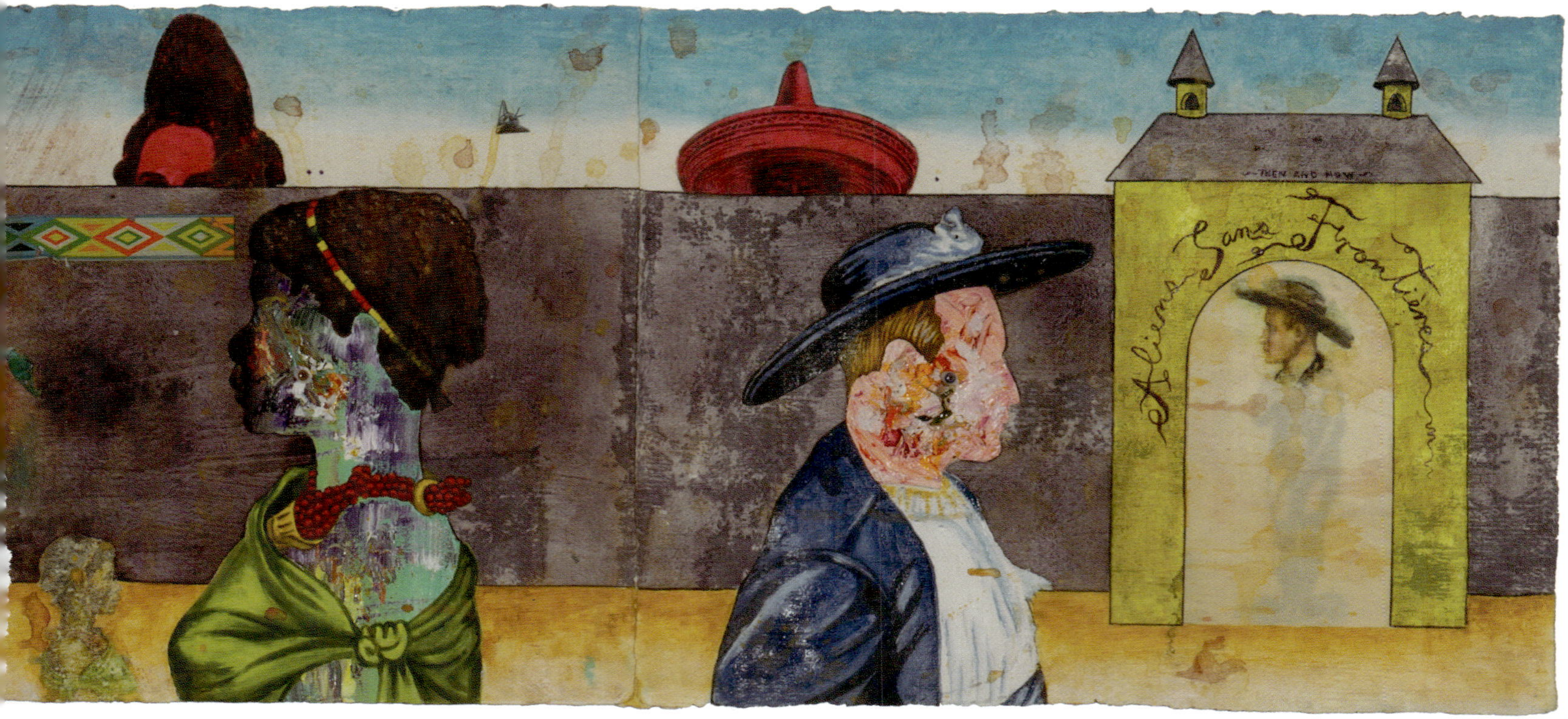

Then and Now: Aliens Sans Frontières, 2018

Acrylic, water based oil, solvent transfers, typeset in Farsi, decals, collaged glass eyes and wood. 11 1/2 x 108 1/2 in.

Words in Farsi translates as “I love everybody” in far left ending panel and “I am in love with everyone” in the middle panel.

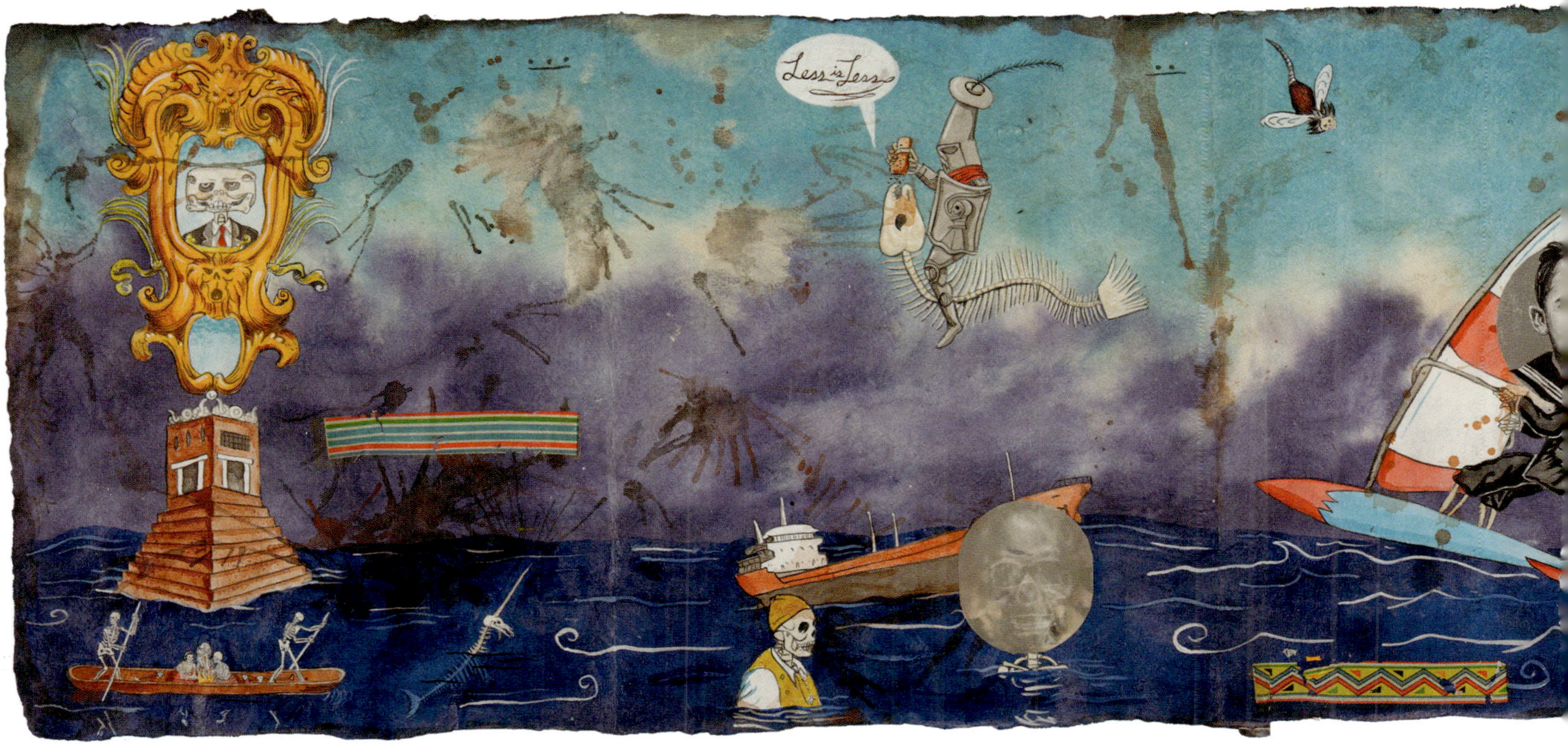
Less is Less

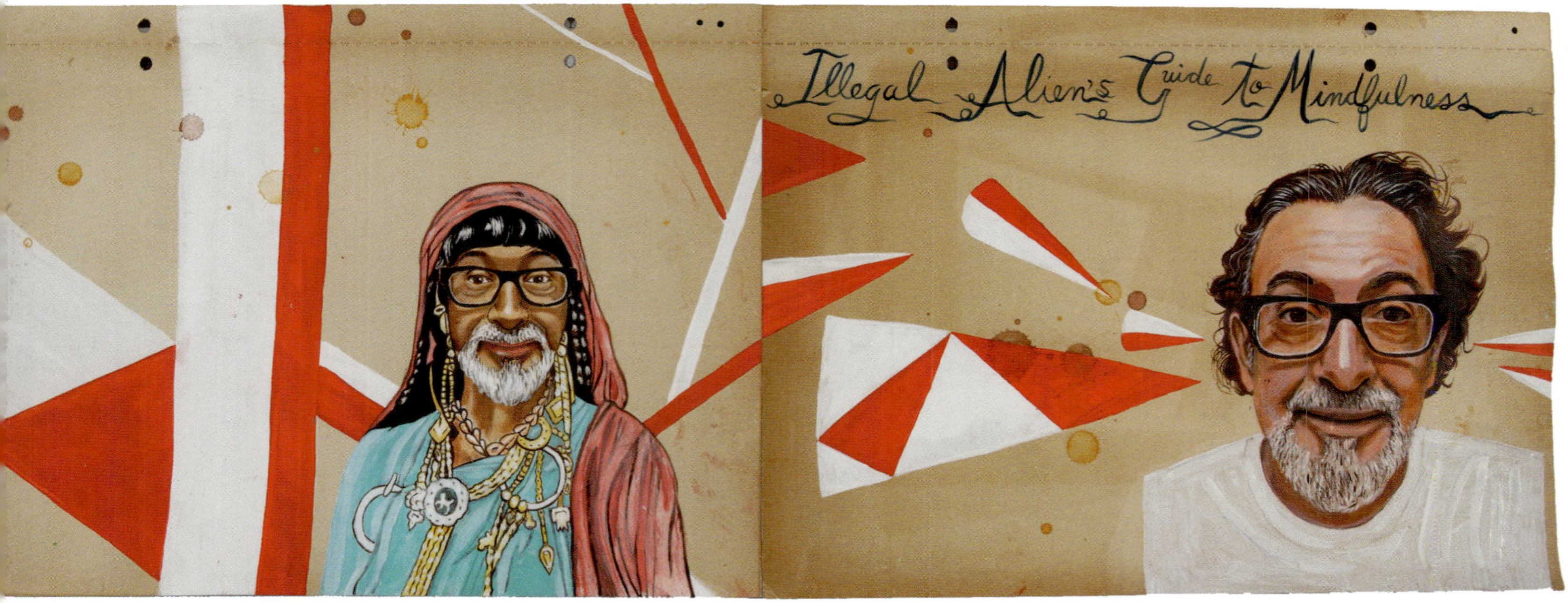

Illegal Alien's Guide to Mindfulness, 2015

Acrylic and water based oil on de-acidified vintage paper. 11 x 96 in.

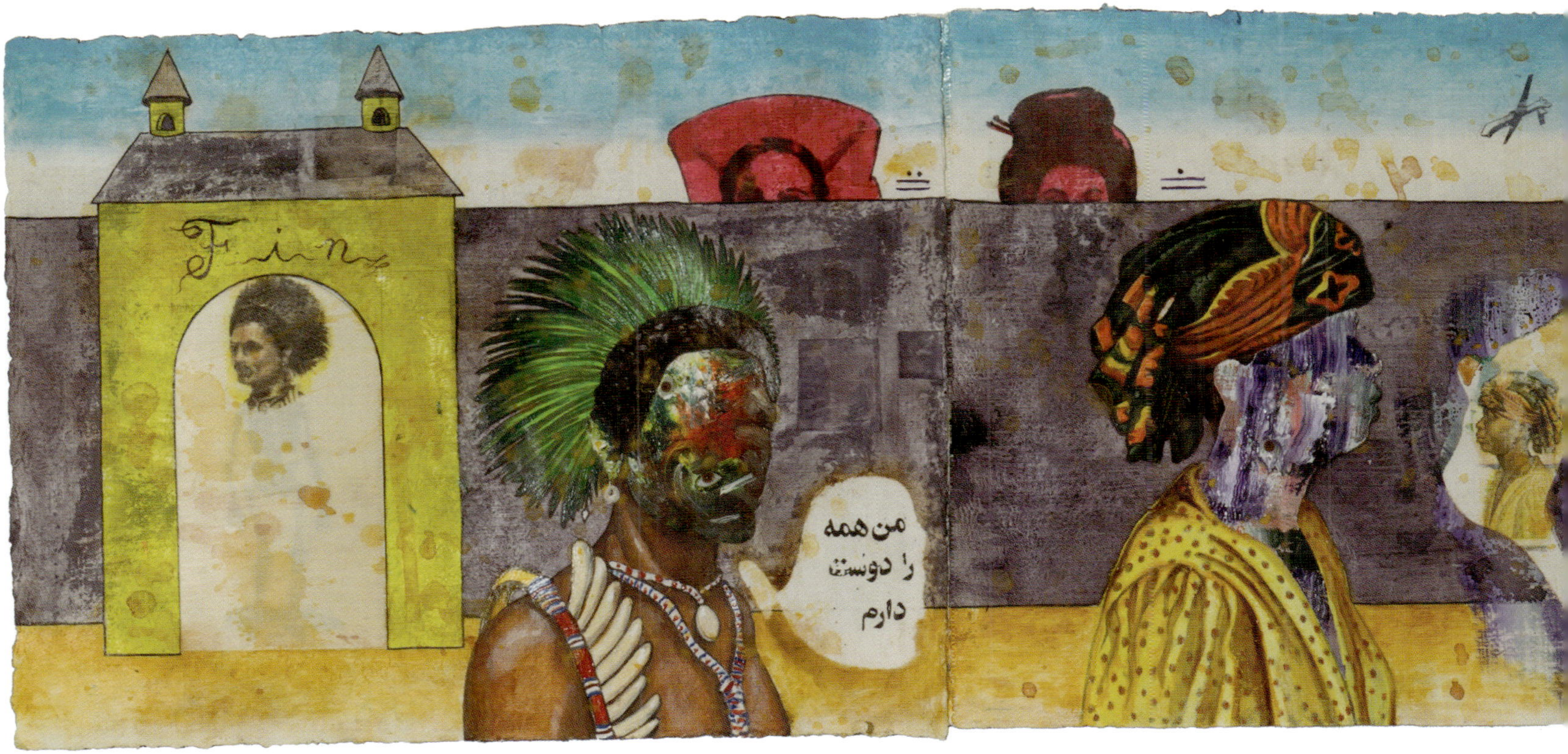
Fin
من همه
را دوستت
دارم

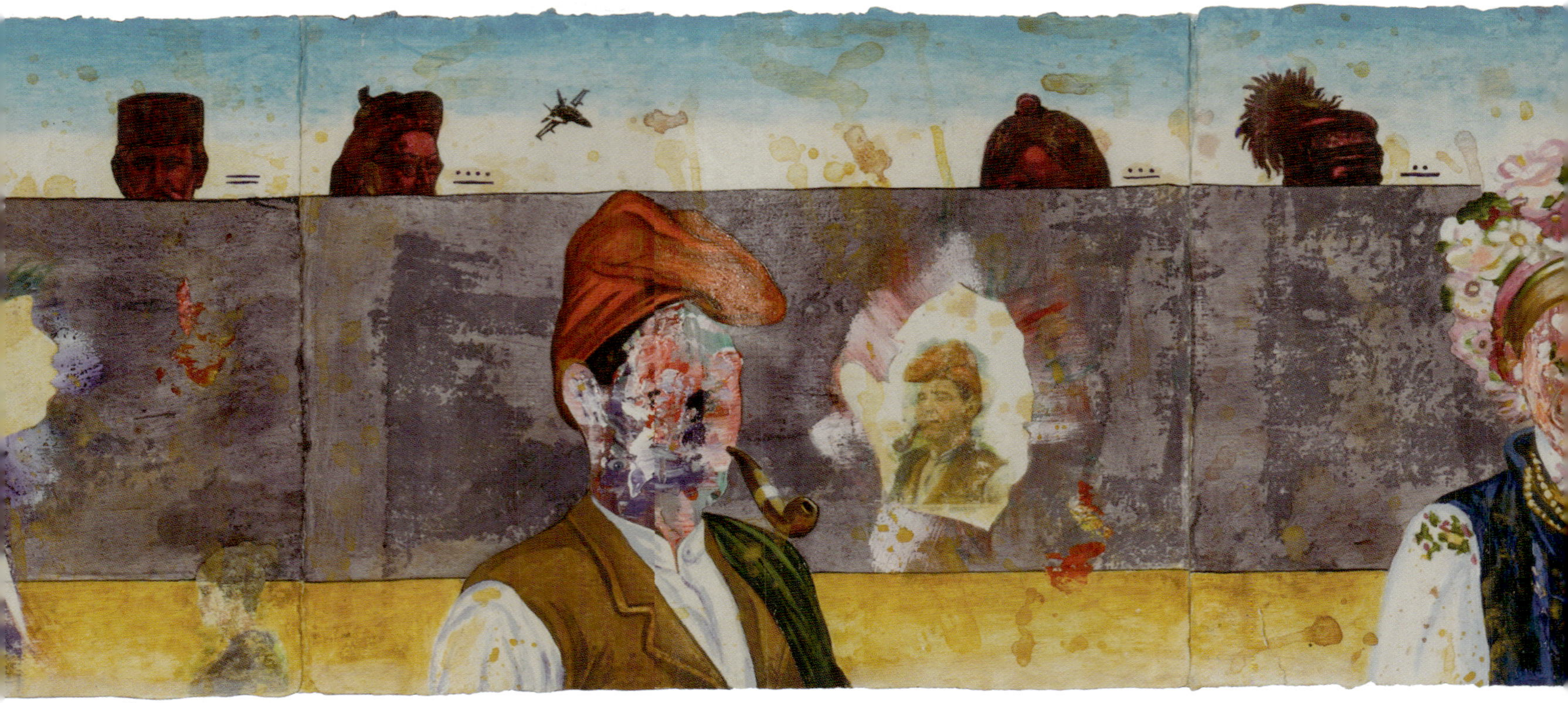

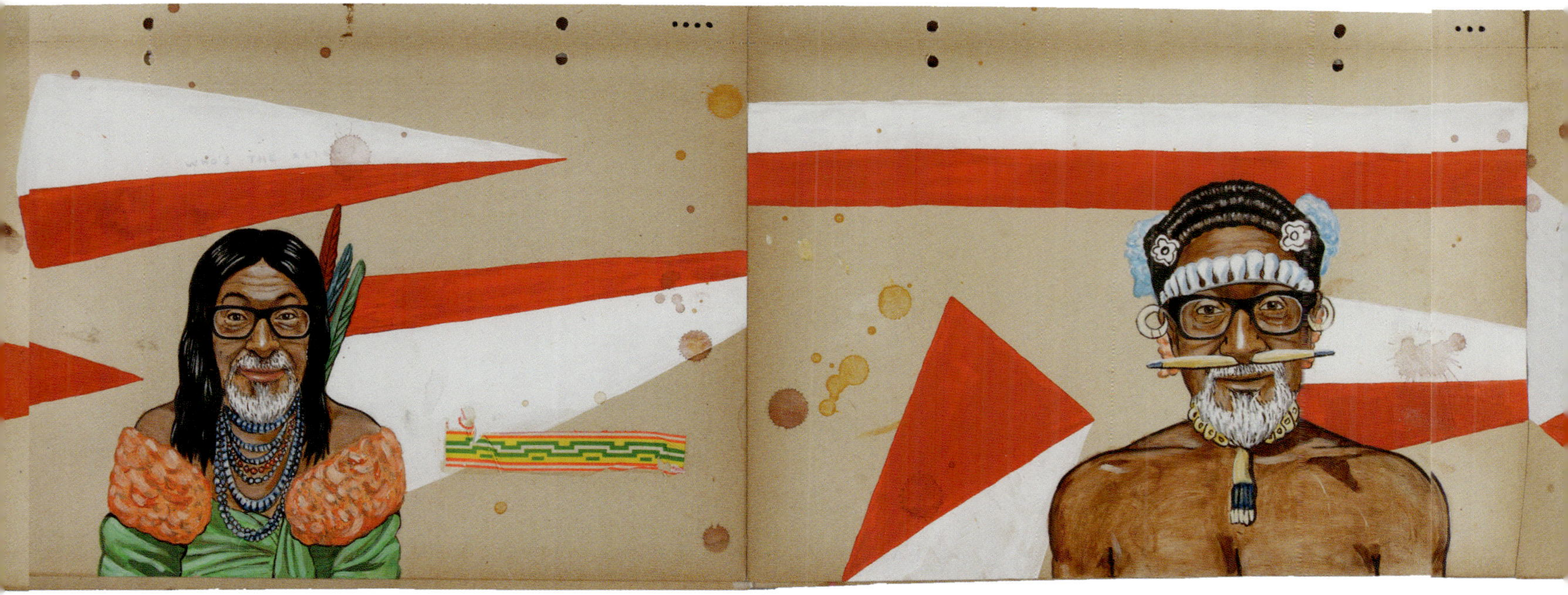